W9-BZL-306

Feed the Need

Need

2nd edition

DR. BRIDGET COOPER

ISBN-13: 978-0692312124
ISBN-10: 0692312129

DEDICATION

This book is dedicated to my loving, spirited, and
remarkable daughters, Jessica and Elena.
May you live a long and healthy life of
fulfilled needs and satisfied wants.

CONTENTS

TRIBUTES

"Life is like riding a bicycle. To keep your balance,
you must keep moving." ~ Albert Einstein

And often you need a push. Nothing in my life has ever been accomplished without the influence and love from those closest to me, and this book is no exception. I struggled for a long time with pulling this book together, unsure of its true purpose and "best" structure. Along the way, I had a number of wonderful and caring people who encouraged me to keep plugging away at it until it took shape. When I left it behind, they nudged me to return to it. They knew that I'd feel fulfilled only after I'd shared what I'd learned as I stumbled along. I know I'll be leaving people out of this in dedication, but know that if you were on my path, you are a part of me and I am blessed to know you. Naming this "Acknowledgements" was simply too distant to me as I drafted this list of people: Tributes is much more fitting.

First, to my beautiful, amazing, and spirited daughters, Jessica & Elena: I know that having a mom who's a coach and who always sees the sunny side of things has its drawbacks, but I hope that some of my struggles have saved you from repeating them in your own lives. I am blessed to walk your path with you and see what amazing women you become. Thank you for teaching me new things every day. I love you madly and without end.

To Lisa: You are my closest and dearest ally, partner, and friend and my world would be so different and nowhere near as fulfilling without your guidance and unwavering support. And this book would be a thought and not a reality if it wasn't for you nudging me and making sure I picked accomplishment over distractions. You knew the book's potential, and your gentle (hah!) persistence gave me the push I needed to not let my passion for writing be sidelined by life and struggle. Your certainty and love brought me out of so many caves I found myself in, and gave me the strength to have this see the light of day. You saw the reality of this before I did, and you guided me to it. I love and am forever grateful for you. You really are my Gayle King. ☺

To Jenn: You are such a light in my life, and my sister from another life. You're the voice of insight, hard truths, and peaceful existence. I've learned so much about myself and others through our conversations and shared experiences. It's a funny thing how lifelines cross, and I hope ours forever intersect, through laughter and tears, smiles and heartaches. My journey is better with you on it. Thank you for taking a crack at editing the second edition, even if it was so you could sleep better at night and not keep pressing that panic button.

To Jasmin: Sometimes people come into your life and the reasons are apparent from the start. With you, I had no idea when I first met you that I found my soul sister, my confidante, and my partner in crime. You're always there when I need you (which is often) and your passion and compassion for others is awe inspiring. You make me want to be a better person and I love you for that and so much more.

To Joe: You are such an amazing friend to me and I don't know what I did before our paths crossed (again). Early on, I was conscious of my need to make you proud of me: to live up to your vision of B. You are such a strong and caring presence in the world, and you inspire me to be all that I can be, which often involves a vision beyond my own. Thank you for being a sounding board, providing me with grist for my author's mill, encouraging me each step of the way, and celebrating every little success, no matter how near or far we were. I've learned more from you than I've taught, so this book is really, magically, beautifully, and crazily yours, too.

To my editing team (Jenn, Deb, Janine, Lisa, and Melanie): I am so grateful for the time and care you showed to my manuscript. In true B fashion, I left you with little time to ponder it, but you combed through the pages and gave the feedback I desperately needed to make this the best that it could be. Your fingerprints are all over it. This book is anchored in YOU. Kelly, my cover designer for the second edition: Thank you for being so in tune with my vision and pulling it together on my tight time frame.

To Ann Sheybani Hampton and Walt Hampton: Thank you for taking the time to write the foreword. I love that we are on a shared path of enlightening and strengthening others.

To those I've had the pleasure to love (and lose) over the years, I am forever indebted to you for showing me where I begin and end, and how to own my own needs so that I can be the very best person I can be. You were a mirror for me, and that is the greatest gift imaginable. And to those who have known and tested me on a professional front, I learned so much from you and your successes and challenges, and from the ones we shared and battled together.

And, out of respect for the negative forces that influenced me, I want to extend my gratitude for the challenges you brought to me that invited me to learn and to grow. The pain and frustration I experienced gave me a chance to see things from different angles, become fierce, and share my stumbles and bruises with others. I am grateful for your time on my path and I hope you learn and heal, too.

To you, the reader: I pray the stories I share made you laugh, think, feel, knowing that you are not alone in this crazy journey we call "life" and that your path is forever and positively changed. Thank you for inspiring me to provide a guide for you to navigate your way through the twists and turns, celebrations and challenges. I am honored.

To my parents, Mom, Dad, and Stan: You have all now left this world and I pray that you are looking over me, seeing how much our short time together has influenced me. Thank you for teaching me so much about life, love, and loss. You are woven through these pages.

Last, but not least, to the amazing woman who set me on this road: my Grandma Dor. Years ago, out of a sense of wonder and respect for my journey and the events that made up the "story" of my life, she asked if I was writing down all the things that had happened to me? She was thoroughly entertained by my storytelling. Well, I did, and will write more books with your divine cajoling. I hope you are smiling in Heaven. Thank you for believing in me, pushing me, and for seeing the humor even in the tragedy that befalls us.

FOREWORD

Do you know how to get wild mustangs to accept being penned in? You build one side of the fence and let them get used to it. Then another. And another. And, before they realize it, they're surrounded on all four sides with no way out.

People with boundary issues are a lot like mustangs. They spend their lives keeping their heads down, avoiding conflict, steadying the rocking boat, bending over backwards, settling for the bare minimum, acting chipper instead of complaining, putting their own needs on the back burner, pretending that they're happy, worrying, walking on egg shells, and selling their hopes and dreams right on down the river. They roll over and play dead because they want nothing more than to be loved and deep down inside they feel utterly unworthy. They believe that if they do everything right, if no one has an excuse to be mad at them, then they'll never be abandoned, or fired. They give up their spirit to others one small chunk at a time, and before they realize it, they're someplace they don't want to be with no idea how they got there. Worse, they have no idea how to get out.

It happens one wall at a time. Solely focused on tamping down trouble, they forget what they're about. Before they know it, they're trapped by a dynamic they didn't intend to create. Soon, they can't recall what it was they ever felt or wanted **out there**.

Sound familiar? If so, help is here. *Feed the Need* is the escape guide you've been praying for. If you're sick and tired of feeling sick and tired; if you're overwhelmed, resentful, and afraid; if you can't remember who you are or what you want, separate and apart from other people; if you're ready to run away from home, quit your job, join a quiet little abbey or a monastery, hold on, Dr. Bridget Cooper is here. She's going to bust you out of your corral. She's going to show you how to take back control of your personal and professional life, one fence post at a time.

Like Bridget, my husband and I coach, speak, and write on the topic of creating healthy boundaries. Walt, he came out of the womb saying "no." He drew lines in the backyard sandbox. He probably took personal responsibility for his own needs and wants by the time he entered grade school. He doesn't always get what the commotion is all about. He doesn't understand why some of us are so afraid to own our opinions or wants, why we dance to the tune of other people when it's the last thing we want to do. But, boy, can he teach folks how to get out of their own way so they can create the life they want, a life of sanity. He helps professionals develop nurturing rituals and habits of success that allow them to become the respected, centered leaders they yearn to be. He spells many of these out in his latest book, *The Power Principles of Time Mastery: Do Less, Make More, Have Fun.* As Bridget says, "If you're not getting your needs fed personally, you carry this experience with you into the workplace." If you want to play big, then you've got to take care of yourself.

As the product of an alcoholic upbringing, I, on the other hand, had to learn boundaries the hard way. I spent a lot of years sacrificing my needs and wants for the sake of others, because that's what I'd been taught. This was part of my belief system. (You'll want to examine your own belief system in Chapter Three of *Feed the Need.*) I'd learned that my feelings were never as credible or important as those of my loved ones, particularly my man. This is one of the reasons I'd followed my former husband to his home country of Iran, a rather inconvenient place for a clueless young American woman to wind up in. So sure of himself, so comfortable in his own skin, so confident in his opinions, his essence seemed an elixir to the rudderless girl I was. He was my perfect antidote, my own North Star. By focusing on his needs and wants, I deluded myself into thinking that I'd never be required to figure out my own. What was good for him would naturally be good for me, or so I thought. Making him happy, I told myself, would create for me permanent security. And when things started falling apart, as they surely will when you take yourself out of the equation, I was quick to blame myself. As Bridget says in *Feed The Need*, "When you aren't getting your needs met, you're apt to behave in dysfunctional, destructive, and desperate ways." Instead of hashing out issues with my husband, defining what was bugging me, demanding or negotiating a solution like a healthy adult, I said and thought the most horrible things about myself. I flirted off and on with an eating disorder; starving myself when I was a little too close to coming unglued; binging and purging when the anxiety level spiked too high from baseline. I abandoned myself in order to remain in a relationship free of conflict. I feared losing the relationship far more than losing myself. All, in a foreign country where I could barely read the street signs.

Now, all these years later, I can still get depleted. I can still grow resentful. It's an old habit, I tell my coaching clients, this putting others first, sensing their needs and changing my plans to accommodate, forgetting to attend to myself, just like them. Even though I know better, I STILL spend a lot of time anxious and scattered, because I refuse to figure out what I need to do to get centered. I look to solve other people's problems instead.

But not Walt. He'll go for his run, journal, meditate, and take the time to plot out his day. He feeds his needs. He makes his wants and desires known, shows assertiveness, has the tough conversations when he needs a reality check, operates with defined expectations and agreements, honors his own time and energy. He doesn't run himself ragged, betray his own interests, try too hard to make others like him, have a hard time saying no, or give away the shop for free. He doesn't allow resentment to build until he's forced to pull the plug on a situation or a relationship. So when the sh*t hits the fan for clients, or family members, or friends, he's there for them, fixing what needs to be fixed, staying steady through the storm. Because he's fed his need.

And that's what *Feed the Need* is all about. Identifying your own needs, and those of others so *you* can thrive. Fail to meet your own needs, and you'll destroy yourself. Fail to identify the unmet needs of other people, both in your personal and professional life, and forget about prospering. You'll want to check out Chapter Two, where

Bridget discusses the four core needs that show up in just about every conflict, dysfunctional relationship, and professional struggle. In each of the subsequent chapters she presents a common problem and teaches you how to identify the unmet need creating it; offers solutions for meeting those needs; explains how it rears its ugly head in the workplace, and how to address it there; and drives the lesson home with some great coaching questions and exercises. If you only have five minutes because you're too busy appeasing crazy people, jump over to page 23. I now teach Bridget's B-Bubble strategy to my own clients with boundary issues. Hell, I now use it myself.

We teach people how to treat us. When you begin the re-education process, you will get guff. People like it when you do what they want you to do. *Feed the Need* is about holding steady through this challenging process of growth and transformation. But here's the good news: you don't have to throw the baby out with the bath water. You can salvage valuable relationships by taking 100% responsibility for your own needs, changing your mindset and approach, and developing powerful strategies. You can fill yourself up, and, as Bridget says, " do the same for the people in your world without killing yourself (or murdering them) in the process."

It's your time. Saying no starts with saying yes to yourself first. When you speak up, tell the truth, get real, value yourself, trust that you are enough, the whole world opens up. The corral walls come tumbling down. Step out. Have a look around. Enjoy the sense of tranquility and freedom this wisdom will buy you.

Ann Sheybani,
Author, *Things Mama Never Taught Me*

Walt Hampton, J.D.,
Bestselling Author: *Journeys on the Edge: Living a Life That Matters; and The Power Principles of Time Mastery: Do Less, Make More, Have Fun.*

Castletownshend, Co Cork, Ireland
October 2014

1

PROLOGUE

*"It takes courage to grow up and become
who you really are." ~ e.e. Cummings*

One day I had to face it. I am a horrible coach. Not to other people, mind you. For them, I'm often transformational. For me, I bite. And not in the good, nibbling sort of way. In the, "c'mon, Woman, when are you going to sit down and WRITE something? You know, what people do when they want to publish a BOOK. Think you could give that a whirl, lil' lady?" I almost got to the point of posting my desperation on Facebook to see if social media could whip my rear end into shape. I resisted. I can at least be proud of myself for that.

Why was I hesitating? For so long, I had conceived of and talked about this book to anyone who would listen. I promised my grandma I'd write a book, and I was on the hook. But actually writing it took a lot of courage. Would anyone enjoy it? Would anyone learn from it and grow? Would I be able to write it in a way that I wouldn't hurt anyone with my observations and revelations? Being the analytical nightmare that I am, in order to shake myself out of this stuck state I admitted to myself that I wouldn't know the answers to those questions until I finished it and could look back on it.

So much for excuses! I decided that I needed to let go of the pressure of being the unfailing expert on everything in this book. Look, I'm a work in progress just like everyone else (not you, of course, my dear reader who is bordering on perfect if for no other reason than that you've found your way to this magnificent book!). So, I'm just here sharing my many stories to offer the insight I've acquired along my road. Plus, I could analyze a blade of grass fifteen ways to Sunday so you should know that I've pondered things in this book for years and years and years.

A little view into my over-analytical (bordering on obsessive-compulsive) ways: Before AND after I send an email, I read and re-read it dozens of times. Oh, and if it's to a former lover (or a similarly complicated relationship), I have to literally wean myself off of reading it multiple times an hour for days after I've sent it. Uh, I know. You're thinking, "You already sent it, right? It's not a draft, is it?" Nope. It's the real deal.

I honestly have no clue why I keep reading it, but I can tell you that after a day or so of this "ruminating," I could tell it to you verbatim. Maybe I missed my calling as an actress because I surely can memorize my lines. So, the revelations in this book aren't fleeting thoughts. I've pondered them for years, and thoroughly tested them with a procession of clients, colleagues, and friends. Oh, and on myself, of course, since I'm my favorite guinea pig.

It's often said that life only makes sense in retrospect. When you're in the middle of something, it's difficult to get perspective. And, it's impossible to see how the lesson fits into the overall mosaic of your life. You can't see how the door that closed opened other doors that led to other closed and open doors that led you down a path that now gives your life meaning. It's a big, old game of dominoes: Move one and the whole line is adjusted.

When I look back over my life, it's been chock full of experiences, that's for sure. Some were beautifully benevolent, and some were downright horrifying. Some bridged both places: with joy and pain. As I look ahead to the rest of my life here on this planet, I know that the future will be much like the past. I'll love some, hurt some, and learn a whole bunch if I'm so willing.

In this book, I'll share stories: Some are mine, some are from clients, some are from friends, and some are from virtual strangers. Some of mine I will claim as my own; others that are mine will be shielded in "Dear Abby" style… "I have a friend" so that my privacy – and that of the people in the story – is protected. In this second edition (the original book was published in 2013), I made a subtle, yet significant, change to the fourth need: formerly "Appreciation." In presentations and discussions after the book's original publication I found myself stumbling over this one and failing to connect with it. One night, after a powerful discussion at one of my "First Wednesdays" workshops, it dawned on me: I had missed the mark calling that need "appreciation." That only addressed a little nugget of the bigger need: *validation.* We need to feel validated. So, I validated myself (and all of you!) by fixing that and publishing this edition. Now I can sleep soundly at night. ☺

And, I hope that when you read over the tributes, that segment that is *all* about validation, you allow my gratitude and recognition to spill over you. There are countless people in your world who may be as thankful for you as I am thankful for my "tribe," but just haven't told you (or haven't lately). Receive abundant thanks. You deserve it!

Throughout this book, my hope is that you will find occasion to smile, to laugh out loud, to reflect, get flustered, maybe even cry, but most of all, to see the inspiration in every moment that we proceed through. If this book has increased those moments, then I will consider it a success. Remember: Growth involves struggle, but it's worth it. So…Enjoy!

"Change yourself and fortune will change with you."
~ Portuguese Proverb

2

SETTING THE STAGE

"If you don't know where you're going,
any road'll take you there."
~ George Harrison

Needs. We all have them. Some of us own them. Claim them. Make them known. Some of us refute them. Refuse to acknowledge them. Pretend that they don't exist. Ignore them as they rear their ugly heads. And, gentlemen, it's not just women who deny their needs. You boys do it, too. You confuse needs with being needy. Or confuse serving the needs of others with being made of steel. So you fail to claim them with clarity and peace of mind.

Many women have been trained to ignore many or all of their own needs in order to live out some martyred existence, turning themselves into human pretzels to "take care" of other people. Other women, my diva friends, think your needs are preeminent and no matter what others do for you, you are still never satisfied (you're the emotional black hole of need).

Men, traditionally, have been told that aside from a few basic physical needs, you can handle everything on your own. In the workplace, you've been supported in making demands for recognition, authority, and control. Women, on the other hand, tend to get rewarded for how we serve the needs of others. The more we give (and suffer) the more valued we are. Or so we think.

I lived a great chunk of my life feeling responsible for what others felt, to an extreme that drove me into despair, low self-worth, destructive relationships, and more drama than even Hollywood would enjoy. I refused to own up to my own needs. I denied them and just served others to my own detriment. It wasn't until I was on my way out of my marriage that I took a full inventory of myself and changed my thinking. I came to terms with what denying my needs had done to me.

I figured out that my needs are my needs to fill. Your needs are your needs to fill. If I come to the table on empty, it's not your job to fill me up. If I need to borrow some fuel, it's my job to ask you to help me, but it's not your obligation to give up all of your own. It was a process, but once I took full responsibility for identifying, communicating, and feeding my own needs, life got better. So much better.

You may have been in one or more of those exhausting (personal or professional) relationships where they suck the very life force from you because they demand that you fill them up constantly. Yet, no matter how hard you try, it's never enough. Their needs are never fed to fullness. You're expected to take care of yourself and them. They seem helpless without you. And no matter how much you give, they want more. They are the black hole of need. And if you sign up for this lovely dance, you're in for a world of misery.

This dance can occur in your personal relationships or even at work. Some of these folks you can spot a mile away. A classic example of this is the diva. Some of these lovely ladies will own that title like it is a badge of honor, something to rejoice in. It is not. It's an example of a neediness that is destructive and pathetic in the same breath, but veiled behind a façade of independence and grandiosity.

Now, don't get me wrong: I'm not talking about the women among us who are confident, clear, and poised and who avoid being a martyr in their lives. Who take charge of themselves and are not afraid to have a voice and a presence and make history. No, not those divas.

I am speaking of the individuals who demand that other people are at their beck and call, serving them above all else. When they say "jump," you're already expected to be in the air. They place themselves in the center of every setting, telling you what you'd better do for them, regardless of if they give even an ounce of attention or assistance to you. Oh, they might be nice at times so that you cannot see the depths of their selfishness. They might even say all the "right" things to make you think that you've misjudged them. Yet, actions always speak louder than words.

They are always quick to tell you what you "should" do, overbearing in their certainty that there is only one way to do anything: *their* way. This covers everything from how you cut your hair, mother your children, maintain your car, and the solution you use to clean your bathroom. If you do something differently than their advice indicates, you're clearly an idiot. You serve them. You support their view of the world by doing their bidding and following their commandments. And you should act grateful for the honor. So why does it feel like you want to scream as they tell you yet another thing that you "should" do? Because deep down you recognize that you are serving their needs to the exclusion of your own. You are a servant. And this feels ugly.

If you're in a relationship with a person like this (yes, divas can be male, too), what are you getting out of it? What needs of yours are being shortchanged? How do you feel being second fiddle, if you're even noticed at all? Are you tired of being in the shadows, treated like your needs don't factor into the equation? This book is all about needs. It's about figuring out the needs that you have and that drive you, and owning your role in satisfying them.

It's also about being aware of what is driving other people and how you can use that knowledge to improve your relationships through healthier communication and productive conflict. What drives other people? The very same thing that drives you and me: getting needs satisfied. If you're hungry, you're going to seek out food until you stuff your face with it and make your belly quiet. If you need validation, you're going to figure out a way to garner some attention for whatever it is that you do or have endured. And, like the kid who is misbehaving, if you need connection with others, you're apt to act in any way that will get others to notice you and pay you some mind, whether or not it's positive and life-affirming. Some people out there are literally screaming with their behavior just to be noticed, touched, and loved. And some will actually die trying.

So, how can this book help? I identify four core needs that seem to show up in just about every conflict, dysfunctional relationship, and professional struggle I've ever seen. These four core needs are: connection (and presence), passion (and purpose), control, and validation.

You might be thinking that there are more needs that I'm not listing out. That may be true, but after you've read the book and learned how to identify an unmet need, you'll likely find that every need that is unfed can be linked back to one or more of these four core needs. If you're feeling invisible and ignored, you're probably needing validation and connection. If you're feeling angry and distrustful, you probably need control. If you're feeling nothing in particular at all, even to the point of depression, you're probably needing passion.

My mother always told me that there is a difference between needs and wants. If you don't get your needs met, you don't survive. Wants are "extras" that are nice to have but they aren't musts. And now that I have children of my own, I tell my daughters, "we do our have-to's before we do our want-to's." This book is all about satisfying our needs (our "have to's") so we can survive, and thrive. Your wants are often so critical, so central to who you are that you are sure they are needs. Pssst…then they probably are needs.

If you aren't meeting your needs, you're slowly destroying yourself. You are failing to live the life you were meant to live. The life you were meant to live is not a life of drudgery and pain. It's a life of joy and abundance. Of growth and challenge. Of manifesting all the gifts you were put here to share and to reap the benefits. Do you really want to settle for less? Do you want to feel unfulfilled even one more day? Do you want a life plagued by discontent, stress, and hollowness? If so, pass this book to the person seated on your left, go grab a latte, and order a fresh copy of this book when you get sick and tired of being sick and tired.

This book isn't just about you. It applies to every person in your world. Again, when you aren't getting your needs met, you're apt to behave in dysfunctional, destructive, and desperate ways. And so does everyone else. We're all on the same stage, together. Your job is to focus on knowing what your needs are, and work toward getting your needs met. It's the same for everyone. But here's the problem: Not everyone is reading this book. Not everyone is committed to doing a self-inventory and making meeting their own needs a top priority.

What does this mean for you? In your relationships, both personal and professional, you will be bumping into people who have needs that they can't even identify, let alone have a clue as to how to get them met. If you want to prosper, you must be able to identify the unmet needs of other people and establish a way to meet those needs as best you can. If not, you'll keep feeling like you're slamming your head into a brick wall every time you interact with others.

I get paid to help people change their lives. I can only change lives when offered that invitation and partnership, so walk with me and we can change yours. I'm human and I struggle just like you and I'm offering up parts of my story for you to learn from, so you'll know that you don't have to be perfect to be magnificent. In fact, the very best we can strive for is to be perfectly imperfect. This means that you can be passionate about a job (or a relationship) that is less than perfect.

Use this guidebook for yourself; for your employees; for your team; for your entire organization. Making a monumental change in the way that you conduct business (and yourself) does not require a full makeover all at once. Instead, all it takes is to make a small change, consistently and with passion. That one small change will encourage more small changes which translate into a larger change with lasting results.

Why read this book? What makes it different than all the other self-improvement, management, leadership books out there? This book is going to help you to identify the needs that you have and figure out how to meet them. To learn how to feel filled up: To feel satisfied and even abundant. And to do the same for the people in your world without killing yourself (or murdering them) in the process. This includes your work life, too. As my dear friend Lisa says, you don't hang up your dysfunction at the door when you get to work: You bring it all in with you.

Do you go to work every day and keep hoping that tomorrow will be a better day? You're convinced that you're giving it your all but you feel like you're on the wrong end of a Dilbert comic. You're overworked, stressed out, you're bringing it home with you, and your relationship with yourself and those with your loved ones are suffering. Maybe you're not in desperate straits, but you know that you could be doing better. Your team has more potential, you have more potential, but you're stuck somehow and you want to be free.

Once you realize that feeding your needs is at the core of every layer of satisfaction in this life (and that of every person around you), so many of your struggles will disappear. If your needs aren't getting fed, you're going to be a problem to someone. If someone else's needs aren't being met, they are likely to be a problem for you. Or they will exit your life. Want the good news? Once you get into this "identifying the need to feed" mindset, problems will present simultaneous solutions: Figure out the unmet need and feed it. Start every strategy session with "what need is not being met that is leading to this problem?" Your life, and your work, will become exponentially easier with that one, simple step.

As you progress through this book, you will find that I ask a lot of questions. I do this so that as you read you can check yourself against the lesson presented, and to see where you might need to entertain a few shifts in your thinking and behavior. I'm paid to ask questions to discover what you want and what is standing in your way of getting that, whether you're an individual coaching client or a management team. In my work as a leadership consultant and trainer, I ask, listen, observe, and reflect. I hear what is under the surface; the threads that make connect us all in our similarities.

I wrote this book the way that I did with the intent of having a conversation with you through printed words and your inner thoughts.

If it helps, imagine us sitting on a couple of beach chairs, taking in the sunset as the waves crash onto the shore, just having a conversation about how to feed your needs and live the life you've dreamed of. It's closer than the horizon and can be firmly in your grasp, if you choose.

In each chapter, I'll identify the problem and you'll see how it shows up in your daily life. You'll discover how to identify an unmet need, whether it's your own or someone else's. Next, I'll offer some solutions to meeting those needs, in you and in others. For each need, I'll share with you how this need shows up at work and what you can do to address it there, knowing that you bring your personal life right in the door with you. For some needs, the personal and professional blend so much that I will address each aspect but not as separately as for other needs.

Finally, each chapter will conclude with a self-assessment so you can inventory how you're doing on your path to having your needs met and living a life with less drama, fewer conflicts, and more joy. Use the book as a workbook, answering the questions and doing the exercises as you progress through each section.

If you have a phobia about writing in books, get over it: I'm giving you permission to write in this one. Go ahead, scribble away. If that idea is too much for you, keep a notebook nearby and journal into it. Just please promise me that you will do the work and not just read the words. I want this book to work for you and you need to work at it for the best results. As I say to my kids and their friends, "we don't have problems here, only solutions. Let's figure this out, shall we?"

Buckle up, put your helmet on….this book can change your life. A little or a lot; it's all up to you. I hope you're reading this because you want change, because there is pain or discontent in your life that you want to stop. And you're hoping that this book holds the key to that. Fear not: it does. But you can't be passive: Not in life and not in using the tools and strategies in this book. You need to show up. Be accountable. Be consistent.

There are no quick fixes, but you can fix things quickly. Does it mean enough to you? Do you feel on the edge of a nervous breakdown because no matter what you've been doing you're stressed out, unfulfilled, and the only light at the end of the tunnel is an oncoming train? Or, can you feel yourself on the edge of greatness and you need to get to it? Read on, dig deeply, and see yourself in the examples. Perform the exercise and do the end-of-chapter inventories. Go out and talk about what you've learned with friends and colleagues. Become the YOU that you were meant to be.

3

GROUND RULES

"Life can only be understood backwards;
but it must be lived forwards." ~Soren Kierkegaard

Before you get started on this book, we need to establish some ground rules, some filters. A few road signs that will help you navigate the terrain. In truth, these ground rules constitute the foundation of my world view. In fairness to you, I'm putting them right upfront so that you can contemplate how I see the world and if it might be a fit for you. If it is, the rest of the book will feel like warm slippers, just the right size. If not, it might feel like you're one of the wicked stepsisters trying on Cinderella's shoe. No offense intended. My hope is that you'll sense enough truth in these beliefs that you believe that the rest of this book will serve you well.

As I do in all of my coaching relationships, I put this information right up front. Love me or leave me, but know who you're dealing with before you take another step. The other reason I lay this right out in the beginning is to set some realistic expectations about what this book can and cannot help you to do, and how you can use it to your fullest advantage. When I conduct workshops, I do the very same thing. If your expectations are different than what I can meet, we need to adjust those at the outset so we can leave one another feeling heard, understood, and respected. Ready?

~Dysfunction Junction~

You've already read that you don't leave your problems and dysfunctions at home. You are every part of yourself all the time, whether you choose to showcase all of yourself or not. Either way, it's all up inside of you. So whether you're at work, school, or recreation, you bring YOU right in there in not-so-pretty paper. As I say in my workshops, you bring your "crazy" right in there with you. The same goes for everyone else. Every client I've had at the corporate level has proved this premise true. You don't stop being you as you punch the clock. No one leaves their crazy at home. If you're not getting your needs fed personally, you carry this experience with you into the workplace. And even though you might be more proficient in feeding your needs in one setting than the other, chances are that if you struggle in one place you do in the other, too.

Knowing this, I've written this book to address your personal struggles, confident that if you get your personal "house" in order, you'll be leagues more effective everywhere else, including and especially at work. And, if you get your own "crazy" in order before you reach the office door, you'll be better equipped to handle other people's "crazy." Oh, and there is crazy. You know it's out there. Everywhere.

In addition to agreeing to that premise, the three things I need you to wrestle with before you hit the other chapters are what you *believe*, *choose*, and *release*. Each of these terms is defined so read on. I'll then offer an overview of how to use these practices to assist others in making the changes discussed in this book. Do me (and yourself) a favor: Don't skip ahead. Trust me. If you don't read these sections first you'll end up in a tailspin of frustration. So, sit down. Settle in. Get comfortable. Soak it in. Reflect.

~Believe~

"We don't see things as they are,
we see them as we are." ~ Anais Nin

First, what you believe can help you to easily satisfy your needs. Belief is your orientation toward the world, toward information, toward other people, toward experiences. What do you believe about the world and your place in it? Do you believe in fate or self-determination or a blend? Do you believe that the world is full of bad people who are bent on doing you harm if you let your guard down? Or, do you believe that it's full of good people who may stumble sometimes, but they mean well? Is your premise on one end of this spectrum? Or does it change with circumstances or simply your mood? Here's your time to journal about it.

<u>My belief system goes something like this:</u>
I think that the world:

I think that people:

I think that I:

Before you go one page further in this book, I challenge you to examine what you believe and hold true. Answer the questions in the previous paragraph. Read it to a friend or loved one and see if they agree. Is that the way that people see you? Wrestle with that information a bit. See if you need to rewrite it. Ask your friends and loved ones again. Check it out and make sure you believe it. Own it if you believe it's working well for you. Vow to change it if it's not. There's no time like the present.

Because here's the truth of the matter: You don't have endless tomorrows. You only live once. At least in this form and fashion. If your worldview is hindering you and limiting your happiness and satisfaction, why not adjust it? Isn't it worth a shot? It's as simple as looking for information that confirms the more positive option. It's like the saying that pessimists are right more often, they're just less happy in the process. Have you ever met someone who can take any situation and make themselves the victim in it, powerless to do anything? It's true that bad things happen and we are often on the receiving end of some pretty big headaches, but that doesn't mean that we have to filter everything through a victim lens. When we do, we attract more of the same.

> Plant rice, rice grows. Plant fear, fear grows.
> ~ Kung Fu

Most of you have read your fair share on the laws of attraction (if you haven't, please make a note right now to do some homework on that). And, according to the laws of attraction, what you seek is what you will find. If you expect mistreatment and sadness, you will find it, as sure as the sky is blue. Even if the person sitting in the seat right next to you went through the very same set of experiences, she might think it was a great gift while you're focused on it being a tragedy. The events didn't change. Just the way you believe: your worldview. The only thing that was different was how the very same experiences were interpreted.

It comes right down to whether you believed that the world was out to get you, or invested in your growth and joy. Even if something "bad" happens, if you have a positive view, you're likely to see it as bringing you a chance to learn something or grow from it somehow. If that doesn't sound inviting enough, just know that people with a more upbeat attitude suffer from fewer illnesses, have less stress, and live longer lives. Sold yet?

Not yet? Would an academic perspective help? In my master's program, I was drawn to a form of therapy called narrative therapy. The premise of this form of therapy is that the way you think and speak about things directly affects your feelings about them, and your future behavior patterning. Change the story, change your life. Have you ever met siblings who grew up in the same house yet think of their upbringings in very different ways? They hold onto certain images stronger than others. They select out what fits their filter about how life was.

But, wait! You mean that the same events can be responded to in wildly opposing ways? Indeed. If when you think back on your life you feel victimized, abused, or mistreated, please do me a favor: Choose a new list of events to think about. Even the darkest of lives have some glitter in them. Start telling those stories to people you know. Feel the shift in your body. In your mind. In your spirit. It's a game changer. You can elevate yourself and move through life with more energy, passion, positivity, and inspiring influence simply by telling your "story" differently.

Why does this happen? Because your mind and body react to the things you say. If you say depressing and frustrating things, you feel anger and sadness. If you say uplifting and positive things, you feel joy and peace. And it's not as hard as it sounds. It's like making a change in your diet: When you see a juicy bacon double cheeseburger you have to resist if you don't want to die of a heart attack. When you find yourself telling sob stories about your existence, turn away from the grease-fest and pick up a yogurt parfait instead. Tell a happy anecdote. Recall a happy time. Live healthier and longer.

I spent countless years stuck in the rut of telling my "story" in a way that just served to hold me back in life. It's true that I had a great number of hellacious things happen in my life. It's just as true that I met my share of angels, danced in the light of joy, and celebrated abundance. When I started making the shift toward telling more of a balance (some good, some bad), my perspective shifted. My anxiety and depression dissipated. I was able to tap into happy visions of my past, which led me to encouraging visions of my future.

This practice was enormously helpful as I moved through and past my divorce. I knew clearly why I left, and I had myriad stories to tell to portray my reasoning. Juicy stories, full of all sorts of negative emotions. And I told my share of them to my friends. But I also told the funny ones. And there were lots of those. We had some good times. We shared some laughs. And I tell those to our children. If one comes to mind as we're doing something, I'd say, "oh, I remember one time when Daddy and I…" They love it. They are comforted, knowing that there were good times. And that I can embrace those. Unfortunately, their dad can't do the same. He's stuck with the other story. The story he continues to tell himself with only the negative experiences. And that can't feel good. And he is in charge of the stories he recalls and relives. And so are you.

~Choose~

"Life isn't about finding yourself. Life is about creating yourself." ~George Bernard Shaw

When you saw this book you may have thought to yourself, "Oh, I know some needy people who drive me nuts. It looks like this book will be the magic carpet I need to get them to change." Or, maybe your inner voice sounded something like this, "Wow. I want to know how to satisfy my needs so I can be more abundant. And, as soon as I figure that out, all the people around me need to do the same." Truth be told, I would love to promise the magic carpet you dream of, but "Genie" is not in my name. As for the expectation that others follow in your footsteps once you've mastered the concepts in this book, I fully support that vision. It's lofty, but beautiful. The truth of the matter is that they may not change one iota, but if you do, you will be happier, healthier, more productive, and more successful.

So, can you instill these lessons in your personal relationships and colleagues? First, no one gets to decide how you live except for you. You choose. So, you don't get to decide how someone else is going to live. Sure, you can lament about how silly, crazy, wasteful, idiotic, destructive, etc. the behaviors of others are, but those behaviors are theirs to display. They get to decide what they want, just like you get to decide what you want. They choose for them. You choose for you. The more time and energy you spend trying to change the behaviors of others is less time you get to spend enjoying the blessings that you have in your own life.

Now, I know it's tempting to "help," but as my father (a self-destructive force to be reckoned with) said, "you can't help a person who isn't willing to accept your help." And, boy, was he right. If I'd listened to him, really heard what he was saying when he said it, I'd have saved myself a ridiculous amount of pain and suffering. I was fifteen, and although I knew he was talking about himself, I still held onto the thought that I was Wonder Woman and I could make things different with and for him if I just tried harder. I thought I had the bracelets and the tiara and everything. In truth, I was holding out for a miracle and feeling super responsible for its absence.

If you see yourself in that story, please don't live like that for one more minute. Not one more. Please. It's such a waste of breath and energy and love. You can want things for others. That's a beautiful thing to do. You can pray for them. You can share your insights and experiences with them. But at the end of the day, and at the beginning of each new one, they get to decide how they want to live. And, some people prefer misery, they really do.

You know these people: They are offered chance after chance to be in a better life and they keep choosing to be in sorrow, in defeat, in anger, at war. That's their "happy." It's where they are most comfortable. And, only if they have an epiphany or their soul gets tired of being so weighed down will they seek long-term relief. If not, they are committed to staying there in that heavy, ugly space. They are choosing to be right about life and how horrible it can be over being happy with it.

Being right over being happy. Imagine that? Have you ever made that choice? I know I have. In an argument, for sure. I've found myself so committed to proving my point that I lose sight of my larger goal: to be happy and loved. So, it's not such a foreign concept that there are those among us who choose to be right over being happy all the time. They believe that the world is a bad place. They behave accordingly. And guess what? It's bad. If they allowed in another perspective, they would be proven wrong about the world. So they choose being right. You'll read more on this in the release section of this chapter because it's worthy of deep examination. I wonder how tight your grip is? But, I digress. Back to our discussion on choice.

Choice is the cornerstone in a healthy, positive, and productive life. Years ago, I spoke to my daughter's elementary school class about volunteer work that I had done as they were doing a segment on community service. The volunteer work I'd done was with inmates at a county jail, both male and female. One of the kids asked how the inmates ended up in there. How I responded was so simple that this second grader could understand it, yet many adults still can't grasp it. I said that sometimes people make a series of bad choices and at some point on that path, they break a law or laws and have to go to jail as a punishment. Other times, they just make one really bad choice to end up there.

It comes right down to choices. It's really that simple. Good decision or bad decision. It's all your choice. Even when you think that you have "no choice," you always have two options, at a minimum. You don't believe me? Test me. It's true. You always have a choice. Always. I will grant you that sometimes those options don't seem like real options. But they are options. To act is always the clearest option. But inaction is also a choice. If there is a gun to your head, you still have a choice. It's not a good one, for sure, but it's a choice.

When you're faced with a situation, you can choose to respond (in a host of ways), wait to respond, or decide that no response is best. And you always get to choose how to respond (or sit in limbo), whether it's with anger and resentment, sorrow and hopelessness, or joy and hopefulness. That is your choice. No one chooses that for you. They may make it hard on you. They may darken the room and make it harder to find the door. They *influence* you. But you can feel your way through that space and choose.

Do you need an example to see if this "choose" thing fits for you? I'm happy to oblige. I call this little story "moldy meatloaf." Grossed out? Don't worry: It's not really about moldy meatloaf. But hold onto your nausea because it will help illustrate the moral of the story.

Example: Moldy Meatloaf. I was speaking with a coaching client of mine who was lamenting his "inability to finish reading a book." As we discussed this, it came out that he has finished plenty of books in his lifetime. Sometimes it only takes him two or three days to blast through a book. So his statement was factually wrong. He isn't unable to finish a book. I wondered if the difference was subject matter or genre? Nope. He'd read nonfiction and fiction books cover-to-cover as much as he'd stopped reading them mid-stream.

After pointing out the lie he was telling himself (that he doesn't finish books when he clearly has finished a large pile of them), I asked him why he tends to stop a book in the middle. He described a few reasons: Subject matter was boring, repetitive, or just didn't hold his interest. Okay, now we were getting somewhere.

Instead of congratulating himself for not wasting more of his precious time on lousy reads and rather than criticizing the unskilled authors, he owned it as his "failure." I threw out a hypothetical case to him: Pretend he and I were good friends. We were honest with one another and never faked a thing. One night he comes to my house for dinner and I serve him meatloaf. He's heard all about my famous meatloaf and is excited to try it.

At first he's enjoying it. He gets about midway through the slice and notices that there is mold all over the remaining half. Ewwwww. What would he do? Would he smile pretty and eat it? He laughed and said that he'd tell me he wasn't going to eat another bite. I was relieved, since as his coach, I would have had a tough time if he'd said that he'd eat it.

So, why did he feel he had to finish a book that was bad? I thought maybe it was the wasted money, but he gets his books from the library. What was it? We concluded that when he chose to "quit" he thought that made him a "quitter." That somehow, if he chose to start something he had to choose to not only continue it but also to finish it. You might be thinking, "yeah, of course. You're supposed to finish what you start." Okay, fair enough. That sounds great on paper. But what if it's moldy meatloaf? Are you ready to finish that? Slather on some ketchup and fake it, hoping you don't wretch it up later?

I'm not proposing that you walk away from things when they pose a challenge. I'm simply pointing out the fact that every word, thought, behavior, and action is a choice. Starting something. Finishing something. Walking away from something. You get to choose. You can choose to let the world choose for you. That's a choice, too. And there are consequences to every choice (moldy meatloaf on your breath, for one), whether you make that choice consciously or not. Why would you choose to waste your time reading a book you don't like? Would you rather choose intentionally for yourself and take your licks, or sit back and be a passenger in your own life? The choice is, and always has been, yours.

So what will you do the next time you start something and later find yourself in the middle of it, without any motivation to do anything more? Will you ask yourself "why?" And wait for the answer? To see if it's something you fell into and really don't have any interest in seeing to completion? Or decide that you want to get it done, using a reward on the other end of it so that you reach the finish line? Please just remember one thing: It makes no sense to wallow in regret, shame, and guilt if finishing it really isn't going to make you a better person or the world a better place. Your energies can be used better elsewhere.

Recognize the choices available to you. Choose wisely. If not, get the ketchup ready.

~Release~

"It's not the load that breaks you down, it's the way you carry it."
~Lou Holtz

Like DNA and fingerprints, we all have things that weigh us down as we make our way through the world. You might be a light traveler, with all your baggage fitting in a backpack you sling easily over your shoulder. You might be an average traveler, with a carry-on and a rolling suitcase. Or, you might be unable to travel because, like a guest star of "Hoarders," you're so weighed down in stuff that you can't even get out from under it, let alone travel about the world.

Which traveler are you? How much baggage do you have? Are you weighed down by emotions and hurts from the past? How much are you blaming past events and players in your life for the troubles and struggles you face? When something "bad" happens, is your response something like, "well, that figures. It's just like when so-and-so did such-and-such. This always happens. If it weren't for so-and-so and such-and-such, my life would have been and would be so much better." Sound familiar? If so, you've got some unpacking to do.

In order to unpack the past, you have to be willing to release those events and hurts that are holding you back from taking each new moment as a new moment and not an echoing of all of the bad stuff that's happened to you across time. You need to loosen your grip on those things that hold you back. And, tougher still, you need to let go. Ready?

There are a few key elements in the release process. They all are critical to releasing yourself from the burdens of things that have happened. There is no magic wand. It's going to take work. Please be aware that the last one is the hardest for most people, so I need to stretch your muscles before we get to the "f" word. They key elements are: Push, Prosper, and Forgive (ooooh).

~*Push*~

"Nobody can hurt me without my permission."
~ Mahatma Gandhi

One of the biggest issues I encounter with people is the challenge in figuring out what their baggage is and what belongs to someone else. When you have boundary issues it's a huge challenge to figure out what is your baggage and what belongs to someone else. You either blame others for all of the problems in your life or you take on everybody's troubles as if they were your own.

You want more happiness and less stress? It comes down to the simplest task: creating boundaries. Letting other people own their "stuff" while you own yours.

When you have firm boundaries you can sit back and observe as others run around you in a state of utter craziness. Imagine the power. You don't feel the crazy. You don't try to fix the crazy. You may try to open the window to let some crazy out, or maybe comment on the crazy to make sure that you've done your part to demonstrate your awareness of the dance. You hear the music, but your feet stay still. You *can* resist taking on drama that does not belong to you. You can resist trying to fix others or their situation. You recognize that they must be meeting some need to continue with this ridiculous behavior. But you feed your needs in other ways, so you can just watch without entering the fray.

Have you seen someone with a strong sense of Mine vs. Yours? Who stands there and just observes without participating?

Before I got the hang of boundaries, I thought people like that – who stayed "detached" and out of the drama – must be drugged, numbed out to the world. Now I am the one considered suspect.

At one holiday function my sister asked me what I was "on" because I was so calm. She couldn't understand that I was high on boundaries. I was in what I have affectionately come to call my "B-Bubble" (pronounced "Buh Bubble" for those audio book lovers out there). Like being in an impenetrable bubble, when I'm in my B-Bubble, the crazy, anxiety-provoking, maddening behavior that others display just bounces right off the surface and isn't allowed into my mental space. I'm a very visual person, so sometimes I revel in imagining their craziness ricocheting off the Plexiglas, and splashing back onto them.

Perhaps you would like to use this tactic. Change the first letter of B-Bubble to the first letter of your name ("J-Bubble" or "E-Bubble," for example). Imagine their chagrin when what they thought was going to burst your bubble flies right back at them? It's strangely satisfying to experience other people having to hold their own anxiety and negative behaviors and not able to take them out on you. And it's surprisingly soothing for those around you; I have learned this for myself.

Awhile back, I was at a dress rehearsal for my daughters' dance recital. One of the other moms, wrecked with anxiety and worry, approached me hoping to commiserate. Thrown off center by all of the demands and the perfectionist dance instructor, she was floored by my calm. I shared my B-Bubble concept with her.. She loved it, of course, because she'd exhausted herself with mental and emotional gymnastics. Holding my own boundaries calmed her. I didn't add to her anxiety by letting her feelings affect my own. I didn't build her worry tower taller. I didn't offer any bricks, just calm.

Now, before you go thinking that I come from a long line of Buddhist lineage, let me set the story straight. I won't go into the details of my early years, but suffice it to say that I thought everything and everyone existed in some emotionally life-sucking dependence. Where others ended and I began was a foreign concept to me – as incomprehensible as walking upside down on the ceiling. I was a poster child for co-dependence for a long, long, LONG time.

So I now reap a great deal of satisfaction from being able to resist jumping in and trying to fix everything.

I say, "Oh" a lot. As in, "Oh, you seem upset." Or, "Oh, you look mad about that." And, "Oh, you seem bothered by what's going on."

What did I used to say? Things like: "I'm sorry, I didn't mean to do that." Or, "I'm sorry, what can I do to fix that?" And, "You poor thing, what can I give you to make you feel better?" (Do you recognize yourself?)

On the surface, these may seem like caring things to say. And they are. But only if you're not taking on the responsibility for making others feel better. That's on them. That is their job to own. You own your contribution, they own the final result.

Healthy relationships are like that: You own your stuff and I own mine. And we talk about the acreage in the middle of us, the relationship that joins us together. I don't try to squish myself into your bubble or suck you into mine. We are individuals, with unique experiences and feelings and thoughts. I don't own yours, and you don't own mine. And you can be upset, and I don't have to fix it. I don't have to assume responsibility for your hurt or anger; however, I can (and must) if it's partly mine. Under no circumstances do I claim responsibility in order to make you feel better. That does you absolutely no favors.

Years ago, as I was getting back into the dating scene, I read a book that forever changed my life: "Fearless Loving" by Rhonda Britton. As a result of this book, I took ownership of my needs in a relationship. One of the exercises in her book instructed me to come up with a list of what I was looking for (my needs) and challenged me to never compromise on the "Top 5." They were deal breakers. Do not pass "go," do not collect $200, stop-right-there-features.

And I put them to the test. I not only carried them in my mind, but I discussed them openly. As I got into a relationship with someone and we started that "what are you looking for" conversation, I had my five and I made them known. I put them right out there. When it became clear after some time spent getting to know the other person and our "fit," I would have that "talk" and they always knew which one (or ones) of the five that were not "there" in the relationship.

Why was this important? Because I took full responsibility for my needs and didn't lapse back into a pattern of taking on their frustration or disappointment as my own or something I had to "fix." Since I'm still in contact with nearly every one of those men, I'm guessing that this approach wasn't a bad one. We faced, as adults, why it wasn't working, and, why it wasn't going to work if there wasn't a shift. For me, it felt empowering to own my needs and not be apologetic for them. To know that it was okay to need what I needed and it didn't have to mean that either one of us was wrong if we didn't make a "love connection." Just that we didn't fit. And that is ok.

That book and those exercises taught me a very important life lesson: That I have my needs and my issues, and other people have their own. I have the responsibility to own mine and I have no business getting into their drama. In a relationship, I can choose to try to feed their needs and help them with things in their life, but it's not on my shoulders. And the reverse is true. And when I stay in that bubble and don't let the unhealthy and destructive patterns and demands of others to get into my head and my heart, I preserve myself for people who won't behave in that way. If I let them into my bubble, I risk being too exhausted and unhealthy to do anyone any good.

Are you ready to get in your own bubble? Nose plug or boundaries: it's your pick. Your Bubble is really cozy, and it's not lonely. As a matter of fact, your relationships will become more genuine and deeper because you won't be drawn into feeling guilty and responsible for problems that aren't yours. And you won't be burdening others with your baggage. Instead, you'll be seeing more clearly what belongs to you and what belongs to the other person so that you can relate to one another in a respectful and non-dramatic fashion.

Drama comes from people being outside of their bubble. I equate drama-based situations to the plant in "Little Shop of Horrors": if you feed it, it just grows bigger and bigger. If you stay in your bubble when someone creates drama, you don't feed it. Unlike some of our other needs, drama-seeking behavior should not be rewarded with attention or it just breeds more of it. Resist the urge to add to it.

Instead, stay in your bubble, and observe the dramatic behavior. Determine the "actor's" unmet need, and see if you can find a strategy to fill it in a less destructive and draining way.

I've found that the unmet need is usually connection and trying to feed that need with drama is highly ineffective, but heavily relied upon for some folks out there. They won't own their real need, so they create a whole heap of drama to get attention. Instead of reacting aggressively toward the drama, find another way to have the person feel connected to others that doesn't make you want to take a Xanax. Or pick up a baseball bat. Neither of those options, despite how much they may temporarily satisfy you, is optimal.

~*Prosper* ~

"Whether you think you can, or you think you can't:
you're right." ~Henry Ford

In order to leave the past in the past and to take on new moments as new moments, you have to come from a place of wanting to prosper and living in joy and gratitude. At its core, wanting to prosper at a human level is about preferring to be happy over being right. Who would prefer to be right over being happy? Plenty of people. Why?

One of the easiest illustrations of this is the propensity to hold onto a low, limiting opinion of your own worth and potential. Maybe someone (or some series of people) told you at some point along the way that you weren't good enough somehow. That you were flawed in some pivotal way that predicted that you wouldn't amount to much. You weren't pretty enough. Smart enough. Thin enough. Capable enough. Coordinated enough. Confident enough. Funny enough. Talented enough. You weren't enough. And some space in your psyche believed those messages and you took them on as truth. You not only listened to them, but you began to live out those messages. You operated under these and you looked for evidence to prove them right. How did you do that? You failed, fell short, and experienced (self-imposed) limitations. You lived their truth about you.

What if that wasn't the truth about you, but instead it was the truth about them? We tend to see others in a way that serves us. We push people lower if we feel low so that we don't feel as low. It's a sad aspect of human nature. People who feel on top of the world typically try to find chairs for the people around them so that they can raise them higher. There is plenty of sunshine to go around up here. People at the bottom of the heap emotionally tend to need to step on others to see daylight.

There is no time like the present to adopt a mindset to prosper. Can you give up the pull to prove them right about you? Can you form new opinions of new possibilities about you? Can you see that you are limited only by your vision of yourself? There is a huge statement tucked in there, so return to it for a second. You are limited only by your vision of yourself. What IS your vision of yourself? Is it a limiting one, or an ever-expanding one? Are you resting in the safety of being right about that damaged "you" that you perceive? Do you feel it's easier to fail (or worse yet, not even try) then to expect success?

Here's the truth: You might not succeed. If you expect success, you might be wrong. Horror! What if you're right? What if you succeed? If you fall short of perfection, of course, but you reap abundance? Would that bring more happiness to your life? You bet it would. As you learned in physics class, for every action there is an equal reaction. If you stop believing those voices from the past (or maybe they are still present in your world?), you will commit a sin against these naysayers: you will be disloyal. And being loyal is thought to be a crucial and positive trait in people. If you want to pay someone a compliment, call them loyal. People like to think of themselves as loyal because we take for granted that it's a good thing. Like any characteristic, it can be good and can be bad, depending on how and where it's applied.

In my volunteer work in the jail system in Virginia years ago, I used to conduct a class with inmates on family dynamics as it related to incarceration and criminal activity. One day, an inmate told a story about his father who used to tell him that he was useless and not worth a thing in this world, and that he'd amount to nothing. He spoke of his father with such disdain, speaking through his clenched jaw. After he finished his story, I asked him, "when are you going to stop being loyal to your father?"

I should pause here and describe myself physically so you can get a clear picture of what this moment looked like: I am a little bit of a thing. I couldn't drop kick a fly, let alone this 250 pound inmate who I'd just really ticked off.

He shot me a viscous look and said, "LOYAL? I'm not loyal to that man!" Undeterred, I repeated myself. By now a few other inmates started to nod and make noises that let me know that they were following my logic. After giving him time for another round of denial to the group, I said, "but, you've created the very life that he predicted for you. You've become his vision of you. You've made him right about you. That's the ultimate in loyalty: You gave up your own life to make him right."

Ouch. The weight of a dozen elephants, and a lifetime of suffering, looked like it rose right off of his shoulders as he pondered this. I believe his response was, "wow." Now I don't know what he did with this insight long-term, but hopefully he wrestled with it enough before he was released from jail that he might have started making choices that served him and not his father's miserable vision of him. That's what I like to think anyway.

What about you? Can you be disloyal? And be proud of it? I've chosen my happiness over loyalty more than once and I'm not going to sugar coat it: it's hard. When you make other people wrong about you they don't take too kindly to that. When you refuse to accept unhappiness even if it's the safer bet, people don't like to be left behind in their misery. You bought a ticket on that vessel: You need to stay, right?

Wrong. If you want to leave your baggage in the past and embrace the idea of choice in your life, you get to choose what you will and won't tolerate in your life. You only get one life. Live it: in joy, from abundance, with love. For you first, and others next. That's not selfish, it's empowering. You can't feed others for long if you're starving to death. It doesn't work that way. Feed yourself first, and then feed others. More on this topic later in the book as we investigate how you orient yourself to your needs versus the needs of others.

~*Forgive*~

"Forgiveness is letting go of all hope for a better past."
~ Unknown

I said it. Well, I typed it. The "f" word. Forgive. Of all of the concepts that people seem to struggle with the most it is forgiveness, hands down. Why is that? For me, it was also one of the biggest stumbling blocks in my path. Maybe just like you, I had some pretty terrible things done to me as a kid, yet I was instructed to forgive those who committed those acts. It was the "good girl/daughter" thing to do. And I was made to feel guilty and told that there was something wrong with me because I wouldn't forgive those who had hurt me. I had such a hard time with this from so many angles. I thought of myself as a kind, giving, loving person so why couldn't I forgive? I watched shows on it. Read books on it. Discussed it with friends and therapists. I got no closer to an answer no matter what I tried. I was stuck. And I was holding onto a whole boatload of anger and resentment. And it was eating me from the inside out.

Shortly after my divorce started I read a book that forever changed my life. The book, "The Shack," was passed along to me at a book club I joined when I moved to a new town. It's a tough read for a parent as the storyline is about a father who has a crisis of faith after his young daughter is murdered. In the book, he comes face to face with God and twists himself into an emotional pretzel when God challenges him to forgive the murderer. Imagine that? Forgiving the person who murdered your daughter? Unthinkable. But then God explains that there are two pieces to forgiveness: Letting go of the emotional attachment to (rage, anger, resentment, thoughts of retaliation) to the offender and deciding how or if you want to be in a relationship.

"Wait a hot second!" I thought to myself. "I can let go of the anger, etc. and still decide that the person doesn't get to be in relationship with me?" Yup. I sure could. And I did that quite a few times after that. As the author set forth, you might decide that the person is apt to hurt you again because they are unhealthy. So, you can limit or even end your relationship with them in order to protect yourself from future injury. And, at the same time, you can let go of the "ick factor" of emotions that tied you to that person. Because if you think about it, do you really want to be attached emotionally to a person in that way? Or maybe at all?

I challenge you to write a list of the people in your life that you haven't forgiven. And next to their names, write a note about what they did. Now pause. Have they done that same thing over and over again, without reparation or change? Are they likely to continue to behave that way in the future? If so, does it make sense to limit your relationship with them? Or is it so toxic that it needs to be ended?

This analysis comes down to an issue of trust: Trust people to be who and where they are and you won't be disappointed. So, if they are in an unhealthy place, trust that and act accordingly. Just like you wouldn't trust your dog to watch your sandwich, don't trust someone who is untrustworthy or you are really the one most at fault. You can't blame the dog for doing what is in his nature and what you knew he was inclined to do. And, yes, people are a lot like dogs: They are true to character. So trust that and you won't be disappointed. And you won't waste your valuable time trying to make a dog trustworthy enough to be left alone with your lunch. I'll leave you with one more quote about forgiveness to help you along.

"Forgiveness is not the misguided act of condoning irresponsible, hurtful behavior. Nor is it a superficial turning of the other cheek that leaves us feeling victimized and martyred. Rather it is the finishing of old business that allows us to experience the present, free of contamination from the past." ~ Joan Borysenko

~Backpack Theory~

Now that you've wrestled with these foundations, read on. As you do, keep in mind that the more that you are aware of what goes on in and around you, the more options you have for responses. And, the more that you practice the options that you have, the more competent you will become at choosing the best option in any given scenario. I call this my "backpack theory." When you try new things, you add a behavior option to your "backpack." You're not locked into a knee-jerk reaction. You have choices in how you respond. You build confidence in your abilities to do a variety of things in any situation.

It's a lot like cooking: If you only know how to boil pasta, when you get hungry, you make pasta. On the other hand, if you learn how to fry chicken, broil steak, and grill burgers, you have so many more choices for responding to your need for nourishment. As you read this book, I highly recommend that you do the exercises, talk with friends, family, and colleagues about what you're learning, and try applying the lessons in your everyday life. Your backpack will be bursting at the seams in no time at all. And having choices makes you an abundantly more healthy, happy, and productive person. What have you got to lose? Just your life.

"All endings are also beginnings.
We just don't know it at the time." ~ Mitch Albom

Ground Rules

~End of Chapter Inventory~

"The difference between ordinary and extraordinary
is that little extra." ~ Jimmy Johnson

Summary: This chapter provided a framework from which all of the concepts in this book emerge. In order for you to understand how to address your needs and the needs of others you must know the author's worldview and assumptions.

Key Concepts:
- There are three actions that you can take to change your life: Believe, Choose, and Release.
- In order to Release, you must Push, Prosper, and Forgive.
- The Backpack Theory encourages you to take a risk and try something new as much as possible in order to increase your response options.

What are three takeaways you have from this chapter? What did you learn about yourself and/or others? What shifts in thinking did you experience as a result of reading this chapter?

Takeaway 1:

Takeaway 2:

Takeaway 3:

Rate yourself on your confidence and competence practicing the key concepts in this chapter:

1: I'm so lousy I don't want to respond

2

3

4

5: I'm okay, but I have a lot to learn

6

7

8

9

10: I'm going to write my own book on this competency

What are three things you commit to do (differently) as a result of reading this chapter? Think of things that will improve your life professionally, personally, spiritually, emotionally, physically.

Commitment 1:

Commitment 2:

Commitment 3:

What are three roadblocks/challenges to being where you need to be? In other words, what are three things (relationships, habits, assumptions, situations) that you need to adjust and/or remove in order to reach the existence you envision?

Roadblock 1:

Roadblock 2:

Roadblock 3:

What are three strategies for addressing those roadblocks and challenges? What are three changes you could make that would reduce or remove the obstacles you have?

Strategy 1:

Strategy 2:

Strategy 3:

"And, when you want something, all the universe conspires in helping you to achieve it." ~ Paulo Coelho

4

CONNECTION & PRESENCE

"Some people feel the rain.
Others just get wet." ~Bob Marley

As human beings, we are all pretty complex. Yet, we hold some essential elements in common. We all have needs. Aside from the basic needs of food, water, and shelter, we have a whole host of personal and interpersonal needs. One of the core needs is the need for connection. We are social creatures and have a basic drive to be with other people, to be seen and understood, and to be known and loved. Not just told that you're loved. But *feel* that you're loved. Feeling like you're important to someone. Feeling like you matter a great deal to someone who cares about you and what you value. That someone "gets" you.

Did you ever have a friend who you could go weeks or months without talking to and as soon as you got on the phone or met up, it was like no time had passed at all? You had a rhythm. You could finish each other's thoughts. You knew what would make them smile, so you did it, and they did the same for you. When they listened to you, they really listened. They heard you. And you did the same for them. That's connection.

As you pass through life and experience heartbreaks, the pain comes from having and then losing a connection. Or, the pain of never having that connection at all. Imagine a life without those needs being met? Sad as it may seem, some of us go through our lifetime without feeling that connection except for fleeting moments here and there. Have you been lucky enough to feel it?

We need to be connected to other people: It's our human essence. Some of us recognize the need to connect at a deep level. Or, you might go through life and only connect with others at the surface. That saying, "too close for comfort" applies here: You might find that there is only so much connection you're comfortable with. And that's what you seek. Comfortable. Safe. And you surround yourself with others who want that same depth of closeness. Oh, you might bump into someone who wants more than you want, but that causes all sorts of discomfort, so like music that's too loud, you turn it down or turn it right off.

> "You must live in the present, launch yourself on every wave,
> find your eternity in each moment."
> ~ Henry David Thoreau

~Connection is Connected~

That's pretty deep, huh? Connection is connected. Wow. I'm pretty smart, aren't I, coming up with that all on my own? I suppose I could just leave it there and hope you get the message. Truth be told, I just wanted to make sure you were still "with" me and not lost in some episode of your favorite television episode. With me?

The thing about connection is that it is such a core human need that it has tentacles that reach out to every other core need discussed in this book. That's why I put it right up front: I wanted you to master the material on this one before you tackle the rest. Because the rest of the needs are intertwined (I resisted the urge to say "connected!") with this one. Connection goes hand in hand with Passion and Purpose. Connection is tied to Control. And, Connection and Validation have a great deal in common. You don't believe me? Let's address them briefly one by one.

Passion and purpose hinge on feeling connected to something or someone. As human beings, we need to know that we matter. If there is no connection, there is no passion, no feeling of purpose. With deep connection, anything seems possible.

Control and its balance or imbalance in our lives speaks to our connection to ourselves, others, and our higher power. Sometimes our efforts at control exist to keep us bonded to other people or things. When we feel a balance of control in our lives (on the spectrum between letting go and holding on), we feel less stress and more comfort in the world and people around us.

Validation rests squarely on the shoulders of connection. If you are feeling connected in a positive way to someone, you show recognition and appreciation freely. When you are shown authentic validation and get the sense that someone approves of you, you feel more connected. It's as easy and as complicated as that.

To be honest, I could have written an entire book just on the need for connection and anchored every other need through that lens. But you might not have seen yourself as needing to be more connected and I might have lost your attention early on. And I know that the concepts in this book are too important to miss. Just know that our connections are at the epicenter of our needs: Feeling a passion and purpose in them, understanding the role of control and influence in them, and the validation of them. As you digest and apply the ideas in this book, just know that if you understand and embrace the importance of connection, the rest will come a whole lot easier.

~Mismatched Needs~

The more obvious issues arise when you want more connection than the other person does. There's that unmet need rearing its ugly head. That itching, draining, distracting, aching, and consuming need for something you don't have. You want them to be your definition of close, and they don't want that. Or their definition differs from yours. They might not even see the disparity unless you push your agenda See, they are happy where they are. Their need is being met. They have enough closeness. They don't require anything more to be satiated. But you do. Sure as the air you breathe, you need more closeness. You want to feel seen, known, and connected to on a deeper level. So there is a disconnect, a gap. An unmet need. And it's yours. And it's screaming to be filled.

You might actually feel it in your body. It might give you a hollow feeling. It might fill you with sadness. Or anger. It might make you feel numb or cold. It might show up in a disease or disorder. Studies have shown that stress has a direct impact on our physical health. Mental and emotional health affect physical health, just like the reverse. When you feel sick or in pain, your mental and emotional health is compromised. You now have three of the four pillars (emotional, physical, mental, spiritual) of a solid human foundation threatened. The only one left is spiritual, and if the need is deep and consuming enough, you're probably doing some damage there, too.

A man I once loved showed me all about this "have" and "have not" struggle. Every element that I described above was our relationship in a nutshell. I wrestled with this disconnect for years, during and after our relationship was "over." I wanted him to want what I wanted, to need what I needed. And although he liked to think that we were "connected" and "deep," it was all a matter of comparison. On the "need for connection" spectrum, he was a 2 (okay, I'll give him a 3 because I am nothing if not generous) and I was a 9 (some days I was an 11.5, to be honest).

It took me a long time, a lot of pain, and gallons of paint (I painted rooms in my house each time we broke up, making me cannon fodder in the "how-not-to-deal-with-heartbreak" joke department), but I finally came to the conclusion that our relationship was never going to work because we needed different things. (Plus, I ran out of rooms.) It didn't necessarily mean that he was bad or uncaring. And I was not demanding or unfair. We just didn't fit. He would never feed my needs. Never. Ever.

Admitting that to myself nearly broke me because I had been in denial and had exerted considerable effort to deny myself while trying to satisfy him. I thought we could find a middle ground and be together. I dreamed that, someday, he would be enough for me, and I wouldn't be too much for him. And he let me think that. He dragged me along for years because I was meeting his shallow need for connection. He didn't want to let me go, but he had no intention of ever coming back to give to me the connection that I needed.

This revelation was sent home in the hardest of ways when I witnessed him enter into a new relationship with another woman. And year after year, they stayed together. I was faced with the fact that he needed different things than I did and I needed to let any image of us in the future go away with the wind, where wanderlust thoughts belong. My need for connection was never going to be met in a relationship with him. There was not a "someday" in our future.

So I moved on. And I was joyous for that shift. He wasn't wrong to need what he needed, and neither was I. It didn't make him cold. His new girlfriend found him warm enough for her needs to be fed. And it didn't make me needy. I experienced that in real time because I never felt "needy" in any relationship after him. We just had different needs. And that's okay.

If you find yourself in a relationship like that, where your need for connection is different, you have a choice to make: Lower your standard (good luck with that), plan to get it met elsewhere (hobbies, other relationships), or walk. Easier said than done, I know. But how long are you going to starve (or, if you're on the other side of the equation, feel like you're a horrible person)?

Life's pretty short and in my worldview, it's not about suffering (or causing the suffering of others). It's about owning your own needs. About identifying what you need and making no apologies for it. You aren't sharing a cocoon; you have your own. You are you and everybody else is everybody else. And if you're going to spread those beautiful wings and fly, you can't do it if you don't take responsibility for who you are and what you need.

"To live is the rarest thing in the world.
Most people exist, that is all." ~ Oscar Wilde

~Me First!~

Maybe it's because I'm the "baby" sister, but I'm putting "me first" right up front in this whole connection discussion. Here's the cold, hard truth: If you're not connected to YOU, you're not really connected to anyone else. You're just a shell or a function to other people. That old adage, "love yourself first before you try to love anyone else" is a complete truism. You must. And to truly love yourself you must be connected to yourself.

How do you get connected to you? You need to pay yourself some attention. You need to listen to the cues your body gives to you. How are you feeling right now? Really feeling? What is your body telling you? Do you have tension? Nervousness? Anxiety? Anger? Excitement? Joy? When was the last time that you paid attention to your toes? Yes, your toes. Not just when they were squished in tight shoes or you stubbed them on a doorway. When you were just sitting down. Like right now. Go ahead and take a minute to wiggle them. Feel how they connect to your foot, and your ankle. Are they tense or relaxed? How about your lips? Pucker them, lick them, feel them. As you breathe, can you feel your chest rise and fall. Is it tight or relaxed? Does it feel odd to be this in touch with your body?

Most people go through life not even knowing what's going on in their bodies unless they feel distinct pain or pleasure. Are we that busy to not even know our own bodies? You bet. We are on auto-pilot most of the time and fail to take the time to attend to our physical selves in a comprehensive way. And sometimes it has to do with what we have done or have had done to our bodies. For survivors of physical or sexual abuse, we left our bodies to escape the trauma. And some of us never fully returned.

Thirty-some-odd years after my body was first abused, I was in a relationship where, for the very first time in my life, I was conscious of every cell in my body when we touched. It was bizarre. I had no idea I had all those nerve endings. It was beautiful yet somewhat disturbing because that experience stood in sharp contrast to the numbness I had experienced all of my life to that point. It struck me that I probably wasn't alone in going through life only half alive. I was not really in touch with my whole self with any sort of regularity.

This was an awakening. And I committed to myself that I would work diligently on my connection to myself, not just in an emotional way, but a physical one. Are you ready to do the same? Can you make it a daily practice to sit with yourself for even a minute or two and just feel what is going on inside of your body? I have zero proof to back me up here, but I have a strong feeling that doing that will allow you to feel when something isn't quite right with your body, long before a sharp pain sets in or a bad test result comes back. And that is a very, very good thing.

~Focus~

Focus, the limited amount or lack of it entirely, is the number one complaint that clients approach me with as they enter coaching. Usually, though, they don't use that specific word. Instead, they talk to me about being overwhelmed and stressed out. About not having enough time in the day to get the things done that need to get done. About being pulled in a hundred directions and juggling multiple balls all day long. They want more time.

Their sleep patterns are interrupted. Some use alcohol to calm their nerves at night. Often their tempers are short. Many have weight issues using food not just for nutrition and not attending to nutrition as they fly from one spot to the next. Their health is often affected, with their bodies echoing what their minds are saying: "stop this train, I want to get off!" Who could blame them? There is little satisfaction in that existence. It's no small wonder that more heart attacks occur on

Monday mornings than any other time. Facing a week of that kind of madness at work makes your heart literally explode.

Does this sound at all like you? Are you ready to stop that pattern? Keep reading and start the process of making your life significantly better.

First, we need to define connection then we can see what focus has to do with connection. In our personal relationships, connection means some level of love or caring mixed with a sense of being known and understood. I used to say that one of my purposes in life was to love. As beautiful and lofty a purpose as that was, it missed the mark for me. I can love people all day and all night and still not feel satisfied. What if they don't love me back? What if they don't treat me well? What if I feel invisible around them? What if they love me for how I serve them but not for who I am? That's love, yet it's hollow and dissatisfying.

What's missing? Connection. Feeling like you and the other person are on the same page. Like you are being paid attention to and you mean something. It's when you feel like someone is holding your hand even when they are not even there. When you don't have that connection, you could be sitting right next to someone and feel lonely, like you're the only person in the world. It's such a tragic feeling. Robin Williams said it best, "I used to think that the worst thing in life was to end up alone. It's not. The worst thing in life is to end up with people who make you feel all alone." So many of us have found ourselves in relationships where this is the case. You'd prefer to actually be alone rather than be with that person and feel shut out.

A dear friend of mine has a story that may sound a lot like your life. She and her husband run a household. Their two teenagers are clothed, fed, get good grades, participate in activities, and act like kids do. They do family activities. They have friends. They host and attend parties. Everything seems "fine" to the casual observer. If you dig below the surface though, you find that they don't have any real connection. They have roles, and they wear their masks, and they function.

But functioning and living are two different things. They don't know what the other one is feeling or wants, and they don't seem to care. As long as they tow the line and do what they are supposed to do to keep up appearances, everything is "fine." But emotionally there is no fulfillment. They aren't connected. They aren't loving each other. They are roommates, not lovers. Driving alone on parallel tracks. And this fog could go on their entire lives. It could be enough to live for the image. Or one or both of them could demand to be real. To feel connected, to be present, and to rip off the masks and live authentically and not just for the "show." To focus intently on one another and not the day-to-day distractions that take them away from their relationship.

What would you do? Is this you? Are you ready to take a chance to see if you can repair this hollow existence? Or are you okay to keep the status quo? As with everything in life, it's your choice. Make the best one.

~Build Intimacy…Through Presence~

"Live a little, love a lot." ~ Kenny Chesney

When I had just finished my first year of college, I was home on break visiting friends and found myself at the house of a former boyfriend. We were sitting alone in his kitchen, just talking. I was sitting on his counter and he was facing me and he was giving me grief because I wouldn't look him in the eyes. I would, but for a fleeting second, and then I would look down or away. He challenged me to look at him, to have some sort of a staring contest. I was embarrassed because I couldn't seem to manage to look into his eyes for more than a couple of seconds at a time.

We played this game for a while, until I got so uncomfortable that I jumped down from the counter and left his house shortly thereafter. That moment sticks in my mind, even though it was almost 25 years ago, because it revealed to me that my ability to truly connect with another person, to be vulnerable to them and be authentically present with them, was severely stunted. Why? What was I so afraid of? It wasn't physical: My eyes weren't broken. It was something inside of me. I resisted being connected and fully present with others.

Over the years, I worked at this "eye contact challenge" and this idea of "presence" with varying degrees of success. But my consciousness of it was forever changed by that moment in his kitchen. Now, in my work with clients, one of the core skills that I work with them on is presence: Being in union with the moment and the person you are with, not distracted by the past or the future. Holding that calm, clear, ultimately loving state of being is not easy. And it is made more difficult when there is not abundant trust in the other person.

Through much trial and error, I've learned that you can be present to another person even if they are angry, hurt, untrustworthy, or lacking any ability to be present themselves. To be honest, I've experienced a phenomenal level of peace when I am in that state of intentional presence with a person who is hateful, raging, and even threatening. I've come to believe that this is so because I am not feeding the negative energy and I am able to speak and act with thought and not tangled emotion.

If you want to truly understand the power of presence, try this next exercise with your spouse/lover. As this book passed through editing, one of the reviewers struggled with this segment because it was so personal and so intimate and she voiced that it might not "fit" in this book, especially if you, the reader, wanted to use the lessons in this book to reach more professional fulfillment. I pondered this and discussed it at length and here's what I came up with: If you are capable of being fully present with your spouse at the level described in the following exercise, not only will your need for connection be met with abundance at home, but the confidence and comfort in being connected at this level will carry over to your professional life.

You won't be distracted with your mind wandering away from interactions with your staff or co-workers. You will be able to be fully present. Disclaimer: Please do not kiss anyone at work, unless you're in a family-owned business. And, well, even then, please choose wisely (laugh).

And this exercise is like the connection Olympics. This is not for the faint of heart. Only do this if you want to be deeply moved by the power of your emotions, and theirs. Make sure you have some time for this: you may need it. Oh, and a couple of breath mints.

Exercise

> While you are kissing your significant other, linger. Don't pull away. Stay there, with your lips almost touching. But not quite. And whisper. Talk about how he/she makes you feel. What you're thinking about right at that moment. Something you appreciate about him/her. Something about your relationship that you're grateful for. Hell, you could talk about the weather! Just try it. For at least a minute. You might feel like doing it longer. And, you and your partner can thank me later because you just might find yourselves spending a very enjoyable chunk of time together immediately following this little exchange. You're welcome. My address is provided at the back of the book for thank you notes and gifts....

What is it about this exercise that is so powerful? It opens the door to a deeper level of connection. It allows you the space to be totally present. Your entire physical being is engaged in an intimate exchange with your partner. You aren't scanning the room for the next thing you have to do, checking the score on TV, looking at your phone; you are completely <u>with</u> your partner.

When I've presented this and other "presence" exercises to my clients over the years, my clients are typically thrown right out of their comfort zones. Can you recall the last time you were that intimate with your partner? They couldn't either. Sure, maybe you're having sex, but all that takes is some body parts being put in the right places. This is intimacy. This is presence. Even in the bedroom, distraction is a central part of the exchange for many of us.

For men, they often seek it so that they don't get too "caught up" in the moment and, well, shorten it. Women, well, we have a billion things running through our heads and our challenge is <u>to</u> get caught up in the moment. To actually be <u>there</u>. So, for a man and a woman, you have one person trying desperately to focus on one sensation while the other is trying not to.

See any inherent problems with this? Now can you see how sex has the tendency to not naturally produce the intimacy we need to feel truly connected? And we know instinctively that feeling connected brings joy into a relationship. So what is the problem? We don't take the time. Sometimes, it's just as simple as that. The shortest distance between two points is a straight line. And often the simplest answer is the right one.

~*Commit a Minute*~

Commit a minute, maybe five, to being completely present with your partner. Shut out the world and make them yours. We talk about wanting to be the center of someone's world. That's terrific but in order to be deeply and wholly present with someone, you must make them your <u>entire</u> world for those precious moments. There can be nothing else. No mind wanderings. No competing desires. No distractions. Just you and your partner. Isn't your happiness worth a minute? Or five?

~*Walls and Being Disconnected*~

At this point I need to address a stickier point. What if you do this and you realize that you don't enjoy being (or can't get) connected to your partner. Sigh. This is the risk that might invite you to avoid this altogether. What if you try it and you find out that the problem is not that you're simply too busy for your relationship, but you're too busy because you don't want to be in your relationship? To live authentically and to be true to who you really are and were meant to be, sadly enough, you may have to face this ugly truth. Sooner or later. Because you know, deep down inside, that avoiding this truth is tethering you to the person you thought you were, not the person you really are or want to become.

When you offer the love that was meant to flow from your core, it is a beautiful thing. You are tapped into an energy that comes from your spirit. Not your head or your body, which both have complicated motivations. Connecting with another human being through being present in the moment is powerful (and precious). Most of us are living in every moment all at once, instead of living presently in each moment, and going intentionally from moment to moment.

If you wonder what being present feels like, the next time you're spending time with someone you love, pause for a moment and notice if you're thinking about when the pot roast will be done, or a nagging yourself over a phone call you meant to return, or even what witty remark you're going to say next. Being present truly means indulging in the joy of the moment you are in with the person you are with and not contemplating past or future events. You're giving yourself openly and completely to the person with you. There is nothing more precious.

Most of us find ourselves not being present because we're under the illusion that we're too busy. I work with my clients on time management issues so that they can fit in all of their activities into a narrow band of time. They want to know how to multi-task, and live in their over-scheduled days without consequence. I give them all that I can in the way of tools, but being present and in deep connection with others surely gets lost in that shuffle.

The walls we build in our relationships keep the fear and lack of trust intact. They protect us from being hurt, disappointed, rejected, and embarrassed. We respect the utility of these walls so we keep them impenetrable, especially if they were built or strengthened in response to a heart break. One of the greatest problems with these walls is that they not only keep other people out, but they keep us in.

When I am invested in keeping up my defenses, the "real" me cannot emerge. I am hidden from view and my core purpose to connect and share my spirit with other people is truncated. Being deaf or blind has been equated to being in a prison of sorts, unable to access one of our senses to connect with life on every possible level.

When our hearts are obscured by our defenses, we are in a prison of our own design.

Over and over again in my life I've been in relationships with people (okay, men), who were hiding their hearts. Locked away in an emotional and spiritual prison. Some were stuck in this place temporarily, while for others it seemed like a way of life. At some early point in life, I received the message that it was my job to bring healing to others.

It's an inspirational purpose, really, but the complication was that I was supposed to overcome their objections to receiving the help I was so energetically offering to them. I became an emotional Sumo wrestler cross-bred with an impassioned litigator. I would try to love them out of their stuck state, and deliver convincing (at least to me!) orations on why letting their guard down with me was like winning the spiritual lottery. Most remained unconvinced. I had not only failed to bring happiness and connection to my life, but to theirs as well. One painful "failure" stood on the shoulders of the one before, compounding the grief.

The grief we feel when we lose someone we love… through departure, disagreement, or death…is not fresh, it draws from previous losses. We relive the similarities of each subsequent loss and they can build one on top of the next. It's no small wonder that we build walls to insulate us from connection. We believe, even if we do so subconsciously, that if we are not connected that we won't feel loss and pain. Nothing could be further from the truth. Because behind those walls, there is a constant reminder of the original loss and pain. Those experiences are the bricks and the mortar, and we can keep them strong only by reliving those injuries in our minds and hearts. We experience the pain over and over again to convince ourselves and others why we keep the walls intact.

It is a tremendous blessing when you meet someone and you connect with them in a deep way. You recognize their humanity and offer yours to them: your strengths and the frailties we are often encouraged to cloak…we give them the whole enchilada. We surrender. In that surrender, we are showing a tremendous strength, knowing that no relationship comes with a guarantee. If we are living with passion and intent, with a little practice, the surrender comes naturally. Being strong in our vulnerability feels right and we know we are real. Why, then, is there so much angst in our personal relationships?

~*Tackle Fear*~

It's simple. Fear. Fear cripples us. Fear erodes trust. Trust in others, in the world at large, in our faith, and in ourselves. This lack of trust paralyzes us and, for some, fosters intense feelings of anger and hopelessness. Relationships based on mistrust, fear, anger, hopelessness, and other negative emotions bring us further and further away from living lives of passion. There is no room for being authentic, and without that realness we are removed from our very humanity.

I struggled for years with a deep fear and lack of trust in everything and everyone. I had what I call a "colorful" upbringing and I was deeply scarred in places. I felt abandoned and craved connection. I would rush into and then cling to relationships that nearly destroyed me on every level. Regardless of who my lover was, the relationships eventually broke apart. I didn't trust anyone, especially not myself. What did I do to attempt to bring some calm and relief to myself? I tried to control every aspect that I could: Every word I said, how I looked, what I accomplished, and anything I could figure out that would make me feel safer within the relationship. Did this help? Indeed. It calmed some of the fear and increased some of the trust because less was left to chance.

What did I learn from this (aside from identifying the need to seek some therapy and leave that garbage in my past)? That there is a clear and solid connection between fear and trust and the need to exert control. And, that there is a mitigating influence on that dynamic: Relationship building. It's really the only thing that can reduce fear, increase trust, and invite a reduction of control mechanisms. When people are in positive, healthy relationships, trust increases and fear decreases. As a direct result, control can dissipate. Over the years, I found this same dance existing in both personal and professional dynamics and knew it was time to develop a model that I could use to illustrate it. It is depicted in the image below.

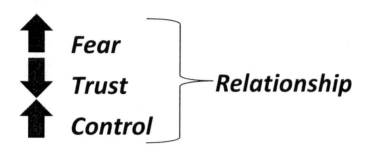

Dr. Bridget Cooper, Pieces In Place, 2013

~Influence It~

So the big question is, how do you go about influencing this dynamic? What can you do with your relationships that will have a positive impact on the mixture of fear, trust, and control? When I coach groups of front-line staff who bear the brunt of the complaints a company receives, we start with an agreement that we will have a relationship (not a content) focus. What do I mean by a relationship (vs. content) focus?

Let's say that the person on the other end of the phone is completely wrong about something. A content-focused response would be to point out the error and try to get the person to admit their error. A relationship-focused response would beg the question as to whether or not discussing the error would put the relationship in a better or worse place? If better, then the issue would be addressed. If worse, it would be overlooked, or at the very least, softened so that the person on the receiving end left the conversation feeling valued, respected, and cared about. Again, the bottom line is the relationship. As the relationship builds, trust increases, fear decreases, and control mechanisms relax their stronghold.

Want to know the key secret in establishing trust and ensuring that you are met with as little resistance as possible? It's easy. Validate the other person. Resist the urge to tell the person that they "shouldn't" feel a certain way. Let them know that you understand why they feel the way that they feel. And allow them to feel sad or mad. It's okay for them to "feel the suck." They will move forward, in their own, sweet time. But more about that in the Validation chapter later in this book.

And it's also about boundaries. Don't get your stuff all wrapped up in their stuff: The issue is not whether or not YOU would feel that way. They feel that way and that's enough. Validate them. Acknowledge their experience, their pain. Then, and only then, attempt to share your perspective. It's a whole lot easier to take someone's hand when you're walking beside them and lead them where you want to go than it is to face them head-on, grabbing their hands and trying to pull them toward you.

~Drop The Dysfunction At The Door~

In the introduction to this book, I told you that we are people first and employees second. None of us leave our dysfunction at home when we go to work, though we may cloak it. It comes through the door every day, briefcase in one hand, unmet needs in the other. In this section, I will address how the unmet need for connection shows up at work and how you can address it to benefit you, your career, your working relationships, and the team you are called to lead. And how do you improve your work relationships? Five key strategies will help you do that fast and effectively:

- Turn It Off
- Leave Your Ego at Home
- Show Up
- Be Passionate (see Passion & Presence chapter)

- Demonstrate Validation (see Validation chapter)

~*Turn It Off*~

My life's work is to join with people on their journeys and toward the revelation of the purpose of their life. Bottom line: I help people change their lives. I boil my purpose here into three powerful words: guide, inspire, and connect. Instead of "connect" I used to say "love," but that word is so diffuse. We love in so many ways, and for me, it's the connection with another human being that gives meaning to my existence. Loving from a distance has its merit, but without the connection it rings hollow. And, it's through the connection that I am able to guide and to inspire. Without it, it's just words on a sheet of paper.

And that's a danger of our electronic age. We are fast forgetting how to connect. How many times have you seen a table full of "friends" who are texting or doing something else on their phones and not even looking at each other? How connected do you think the people at the table feel to one another? How about to the people they are texting? Is that really the deep connection that you are looking for?

It might suffice, but it leaves you feeling empty and like you are floating through life, not firmly at the wheel, guiding you haphazardly to your intended destination. I liken it to clouds. You exist in a world full of wispy, clustered clouds that spread and move without notice. And tiptoeing through life like that isn't for me. Is it for you? Personally, I'd rather be a thickly collected mass of a storm cloud, whose borders are sharp and distinct. Whose formation is noticeable and one that people stop and observe. And whose presence is impactful, powerful, and sometimes even loud. That's living out loud. And connected.

So the next time you're paying more attention to someone or something that isn't even there, stop yourself. Take a deep breath and be where you are and with whom you're sharing oxygen. Be present.

What will happen? Trust will build. Fear will dissipate. The relationship will improve. And control will stop being such an albatross.

~*Leave Your Ego At Home*~

During the insurance and investment company scandals a few years back, I was called in to assist a sales and customer service support staff in handling some of the backlash coming from their customer base. Customers were on edge, thinking that their life savings might be liquidated. They had little trust in the company given its recent performance and the scandals plaguing the financial services industry overall. The sales staff was getting turned away because clients didn't have faith in the company. The customer service staff was being pummeled with complaints and challenges from customers and initiating skyrocketing levels of withdrawals and account closings. Something had to happen before the company hemorrhaged and its employees ran for the hills.

Our team was called in and we developed a comprehensive intervention plan for all levels of the company. My role was trainer. In that engagement, I developed my "leave your ego at home" model. In this model, the front line employees learned how to set aside their desire to be right and treated well and replaced it with the interest of the relationship with the customer.

How did they do this? I brought them through a visualization exercise where they used an object on their desk to symbolize their ego, that part of themselves that wanted recognition, compliments, and validation. They had to put it (their ego symbol) away before answering or making a call or having a visit with a customer to symbolize setting aside those needs.

Instead of focusing on their own needs, they were instructed to focus on how to create trust with the customer. To concentrate on listening without defending. To place themselves in the customer's shoes and acknowledge the customer's frustration. Not to figure out how to be right or understood or to win any part of any argument. The goal was only to create a good relationship with the customer. I call this the "Invested Detachment" model: You're invested in the relationship, but detached from your personal stake and ego. It's holding on and letting go at the same time. It's controlling what you can and releasing what you cannot.

And, returning to the Fear-Trust-Control model, they were addressing the relationship in order to reduce fear, increase trust, and impact the customer's control efforts (which included taking their money elsewhere). I'm happy to report that this company survived that rocky time, due in no small part to the mental shift and behavioral changes by its employees to address a novel issue in the history of the company: A massive loss of trust, and fear being at an all-time high in the industry.

So what can you learn from that company? How can you use the ego exercise to benefit your job and your organization? It's simple, really. Try it for yourself. The next time you're faced with a problem with a client, shift quickly into a relationship-focus. Ask yourself what you could do to create more trust in the relationship. Offer answers and follow-up, and do so right away. Under promise and over deliver. Take baby steps toward creating a trusting relationship. Resist the urge to prove that you're right, even if you are. Put your energy into making your client (internal or external) feel good.

Once the customer starts to trust you more, they will fear less and let go of some of their efforts to control the process. If you try to convince them to trust more or fear less, your words will fall on deaf ears. You must show them that they would be right to trust you more and to let go of some of their fear. You can't try to take away control (denying their requests, etc.). If you do, they will just find new ways to do so because when you are in a state of fear and distrust, you will go to any lengths to control something, or risk going crazy. You have to focus on the connection with the client. It's all in the connection. We do business and takes risks with those we feel connected to and trusting toward. Want more business? Get and stay more connected.

~*Show Up* ~

A great number of my clients struggle to feel connected at work, and it brings them considerable unrest when they don't feel it. If you're feeling a lack of connection at work, is it because you don't feel interpersonal satisfaction with the people you work with? Or is it that you don't feel connected to the work itself? Do you come and go each day, just taking up space, pushing through task after task and meeting after meeting? Can you remember the last time you smiled on your way into work? Is work just drudgery and obligation? For so many people, their job is just a way to make a paycheck and have health insurance.

Chances are, even if you're connected to some of the people you work with, you may not be connected to your job. That's something to be sad about. It's depressing, really, because you probably spend more time at work than you do anywhere else. Not to mention the time you spend when you're *doing* something else but you're *thinking* about work. That's a big chunk of your life spent on something that isn't bringing you great pleasure. In order to break that pattern, you need to show up. Not just with your body, but with your full self.

A couple of friends of mine demonstrated some real grit in their search for connection to their profession. The first friend was going through the motions at work, tired of what he was doing, and completely uninspired. He wasn't great at what he did because he felt no connection to doing it. He didn't particularly care for the people he worked with, either, because everyone was similarly miserable yet pressing on.

One day he got fired. And if you ask him today what was the best thing that ever happened to him he'll respond with, "getting fired." It was the Universe giving him what he hadn't claimed for himself: Freedom to find work and people that he could connect with. So what did he do with this new-found liberty? He built a company from the ground up and he's never been happier. Every single day he does one thing differently than he did in his last job: He shows up.

Friend number two was in similar straights only he beat the Universe to the punch by quitting his job as a sales executive and putting on his painter's pants and becoming a full-time house painter. His sales job just held no interest for him and he found himself scattered and uninspired, and lacking focus to do what needed to get done. The first few years as a painter were rough as he figured out how to market himself and do the business aspects of running his own company. But he was free of the burden of doing work he wasn't connected to and he now surrounds himself with the people he chooses to connect with.

He is intense when he paints because his work has his solitary focus. He is all about the painting. His relationships are richer, his days are lighter, and his wallet is getting fatter. All because he chose to disconnect from one set of relationships and connect to another. It's not rocket science, it's just risk. And now when he's at work, he's completely there: mind, body, and soul.

The key to happiness and professional success for both of these people was simple: connection. They walked away from jobs where they were just punching a clock and depositing a check. Instead, they rolled the dice and found professional roles that they could really connect with and feel energized by. It wasn't easy at first, but it was worth it.

When they were asked what they did they could now respond with pride, and a smile and a lift in their voices. They are now connected to their work life and they are better for it. They aren't just robots, wasting their lives away in jobs that bring them no pleasure beyond the dollar signs. They know what they are doing is consistent with who they are and what they are good at, and they use this connection to fuel and energize them. And the world needs so much more of that.

~*Master Focus*~

What does your connection to your work have to do with focus? It's pretty simple, really. When we feel more connected to our work, we are more apt to focus squarely on our tasks. Connection brings energy and energy harnessed is focus. Conversely, when we are focused, we feel more connected to whatever it is that we are doing. We have eliminated distractions that keep us from feeling connected. So when we focus, we connect. And when we connect, we focus. And what about these "distractions?" When you're unhappy at home, you're likely to pour yourself into your job (or mowing the lawn or a hobby or an affair). You're driven to find a distraction from the lack of connection you feel, so you replace the connection. It takes you away from the true pain of the unmet need and you try to fill the hole elsewhere.

The need doesn't really get fed because it's the square peg to round hole issue, but it does provide the needed distraction, at least temporarily. It's like snacking on a rice cake when you really want a piece of that leftover birthday cake. It just doesn't work in the end. You're still distracted by your desire for the cake. So you're not enjoying the rice cake and you're certainly not enjoying the cake. Your attention is spread thin so you're neither here nor there.

This is how so many people live their lives every day: not fully in one moment or another. Their passion is lackluster, their focus is wavering, and their output is abysmal. The only thing that is topping out the charts is their stress level: that's sky high. What's the answer? It's focus. Getting focused on what you're doing when you're doing it. How can you get more focused? In the following pages, you'll read about these sure-fire strategies to improve your focus exponentially in no time at all:

- Act Now
- End Multitasking
- Stop, Center, & Move
- Take 15

~*Act Now* ~

Act now. Sounds easy enough, so why does it seem so hard for so many of us? Countless clients present with procrastination as their "issue." Since I'm curious by nature, I end up asking a lot of questions to find out why they are procrastinating. I don't get stuck in the "how" of how not to procrastinate. I need to know the "why." The "why" is what drives us, toward or away, from a destination. So, why? Why are you wanting to avoid a task? Do you have the tools, resources, skills, information you need? Do you lack confidence? Do you simply not enjoy it? Why has it become a monkey on your back?

Example

One of my clients says he has no motivation to get things done. He starts and stops on his path to completing his goals. He gets energized, then quickly comatose. This pattern has sharply limited his ability to reach his full potential. And that's true not only because he hasn't reached the goals he set, but more so because his self-concept has suffered.

We spent some time digging around in figuring out the "why" he has for procrastinating. To get to that, I had to find out what motivated him, what brought him alive. For him, it was spending time interacting with and helping others. That sounded easy enough, only he worked independently without co-workers. He had to work harder to incorporate social connections into his daily routine. When he did, though, he found that he was on fire and blew through his to-do list. When he feels isolated, however, he finds himself with a pile of things to do and no time to get them done. Bottom line: When he attended to his need for connection, he stopped procrastinating. That was his "why." It was a need that wasn't met that was the root of the problem. Procrastination was just a symptom.

What was the disease that procrastination was a symptom of? Isolation. What does isolation indicate? A loss of connection. A lack of attention.

It's easiest to see this if we consider children trying to meet their need for attention. What happens when we ignore our kids? When we don't meet their need for attention, love, and affection? Do they act out? You bet they do. And then we give them attention. And we criticize them because they are getting "negative" attention. We call them "trouble makers."

Truth is, they are getting attention. They are masters at finding a way to get at least part of their core need met. And what do we tell them? We say that if they needed attention (the loving and affectionate type), to just ask instead of acting out so that they get in trouble. And if we pause for a moment in all the conflict, we can see this in our kids.

So why can't we see how we "act out" by failing at things that we could succeed at? How did we get to be masters at seeing our kids' motivations and patterns and not our own?

Time, habit, and disappointment will do that. The role of this book is to take a tour through your core needs and determine how to attend to them and meet them and stop ignoring them. Like your kids, you will find a way to act out if your needs remain unmet and the ramifications are not very pretty.

So getting back to my client's story: Is he right to call himself a "procrastinator?" Absolutely not. No more so than we are right to call our kids "trouble makers." You're seeing the symptom (trouble making and procrastination) as the problem (unmet need for attention, personal connections, etc.). Treat the problem (the unmet need), not the symptom (the acting out behavior). If you're getting headaches because you have a pinched nerve, does taking pain killers solve your problem? Nope. It just relieves your pain temporarily. Getting treatment to repair the pinched nerve is how you solve the problem.

So how does my client stop procrastinating? Once he recognizes that the symptom is not the problem, he can fix both. Practically speaking, he intentionally schedules regular meetings with people. In other words, feed the need and ease the pain. He won't procrastinate to create a crisis if he is getting his need met to connect with people. He won't need the drama. And he will feel invigorated by having his need met so he'll plow through his to-do list. And this isn't a prediction. It's a certainty. It worked. It works.

~*End Multitasking*~

When I was preparing to graduate from college and start to make my way in the world, I visited the career center of my university to get some interview tips and tricks. The jobs I'd gotten up to that point were part-time, just-above-minimum-wage positions and I knew I had a bunch to learn about how to land a "real" job. I went through resume writing seminars, job search strategy workshops, and an interview preparation series. I crafted a stellar resume, found every job that even slightly matched my background and aspirations, and honed my interview skills.

And I wrote some of the world's best cover letters. In every cover letter, I wrote about the personal characteristics I possessed that would make me indispensable to any employer. And, one of them was being a "strong multi-tasker." Ah, youth. I wasn't lying. I could juggle all sorts of things simultaneously. You could pull me off a task and have me jump to another and I did so with a smile on my face and a bounce in my step. Apparently being easily distracted had become a positive attribute and a career ladder climbing tool. Or not. I learned over the years, through experience, observation, and research, that multitasking is the wrong approach to accomplishing our goals.

Why is it the wrong way to do things? You thought "juggling multiple tasks simultaneously" was nearly as important as acquiring the Holy Grail? It's not. It's the absolute wrong way to get anything accomplished. Why? Because when you're multitasking, you aren't focused on one thing. You're spreading your focus around like dust on a shelf: It has no mass so it has no intensity so it produces lackluster results (and sneezing).

Studies have proven that when you multitask it takes you longer to get things done and you make more errors. You're distracted, and not just from one thing toward another. You're distracted from each and every thing you're doing by every other thing you're doing. You're not giving anything your full attention and concentration. Your attention is all over the place. You lack focus.

And talk about not having your senses engaged: You are splitting yourself into a bunch of pieces and expecting that the result will be like it was if you had all of yourself focused in one direction. It doesn't happen like that. You have to feel and be in the moment you're in. You have to see the task at hand.

So clear your desk, shut your phone off, close your door, and resist interruptions. Take one thing at a time and do it with all that you have and you'll reap the benefits. You'll make fewer missteps. Think of it like texting and driving: The issue with that practice is that you're not giving driving your full, focused attention when you're doing something else. You don't have two heads or two sets of eyes: you only have one. Do the number of things that equals the number of brains you have to process the information? ONE. Yeah, that should do it.

The next time you're tempted to do more than one thing at a time, hear this in your head like a recording that won't stop until you do: "STOP IT! Just STOP IT!" My other clients have found that enormously helpful.

Speaking of "stop," next are two tactics that really assist you in resisting the urge to multitask and support you in giving your full focus and connection to each moment are done 30 seconds and 15 minutes at a time. Read on.

~*Stop, Center, Move*~

We run from one moment to the next without pausing long enough to focus. We forget what we want (our intentions) to acquire from the experience. We just fly (or for some, float) from meeting to meeting, place to place, forgetting to be in the moment we are actually in. And in doing this, we miss so much. And other people don't get our focus or the whole of us, and the world fails to benefit from our intentional presence. One practice that my clients have found enormously helpful is something I nicknamed "30 Seconds for Sanity." It's called "Stop, Center, Move" and it's a quick (30 second), three-step process for bringing your presence to the present. It goes like this:

Stop   Put the phone down, shut your mouth, halt your movement.

Center   Close your eyes, quiet your mind, call to mind your intended outcome for the moment you are about to enter.

Move   Only after you've centered and focused your attention on the present can you move to the next moment.

All it takes is 30 seconds. Isn't your full focus worth 30 seconds? In the next exercise you'll get to try on for size how this might work.

Exercise

You have transitions from one activity to the next all day long. Whether it is high-profile meetings or getting in and out of the car, you move from one space to another constantly. And sometimes you aren't even conscious of it and that spells trouble.

When you put this book down to go to do what's next on your list, take 30 seconds for sanity. Stop: Stay seated or laying down and close the book. Center: Close your eyes, concentrate on your state of mind, and think about the activity you're headed to. What resources do you need? Where does your energy need to be? What thoughts do you need to hold? Which ones to you need to release? Only after you are taken over by a sense of calm are you allowed to proceed to the third and final step. Move: Carry that sense of calm and focus with you, reminding yourself of the supportive thoughts and those which are not permitted, and go to your next activity.

Once that activity concludes, take a moment to think about how it went. Was there anything different about its process or outcome than other moments? Maybe it's something you do routinely? How was it unlike the "usual?"

~*Take 15*~

In this distracted, technology-consumed, overwhelmed world we've created, we are rewarded for having the attention span of a squirrel. Well, I don't need to remind you that the roads are littered with flattened squirrels. Why? If you watch a squirrel try to cross a road, it rarely runs with purpose and intensity from one side to the other. Instead, it gets part of the way into the street, then seemingly starts looking around for who knows what, and the next thing you know, the minivan barreling down the road just sent it to squirrel heaven.

What can you learn from the squirrels of the world (another of many things I never thought I'd hear myself say)? You can decide to move with purpose, intensity, direction, and FOCUS. Be in the moment you're in instead of the moment that promises to approach. Accept the scattered nature of our society (if you feel you must) and work within its constraints. And focus.

One reason people don't start a project is because they can't seem to find the time. Is this you? You imagine how long it will take and you don't have four or five (or more) consecutive hours to work on it. So you don't start it. It sits. Mocks you. Gnaws at you. It fills you with guilt and self-doubt. You've failed before you even started.

Are you ready for another way? Read on. Imagine that you're working on a big project and you get interrupted. So you don't go back to it, or when you do, you forgot where you left off. You forgot your place. So you have one more reason not to start it again. So you abandon it.

The good news is that you can handle stops and starts if you have the right techniques in place ahead of time. First, set aside reasonable blocks of time to work on a project. If you know that your attention span is, let's say, just this side of a squirrel on a sugar high, then don't block two hours for it. If you do, you'll find a hundred other things to do instead. E-mail. Laundry. Organizing your file cabinet. Planning your vacation or next business trip. All these things are good things, but they aren't what you set out to do. And they are not getting you closer to your goal. Are you tired of getting to the end of a day and feeling no closer to accomplishing your true goals than when you woke up?

Try this instead: Take on tasks 15 minutes at a time. Rather than trying to focus on a project for hours at a clip and then getting frustrated with a dozen interruptions, commit to biting off some chunk of the project for 15 minutes at a time. And do nothing (not even checking your text messages or incoming emails or phone calls) for that 15 minute block except for that project chunk. Give it your full attention. Lose yourself in it by setting an alarm that will stop you at the end of 14 minutes.

Why 14 minutes? If you leave one minute at the end of your 15 time frame, you have time to write yourself what the military coins a "pass down" (a snapshot of where you left off, what you were about to do next, and remaining steps to complete that section). Why is this necessary and why does this intervention work? When you exit and attempt to re-enter a task at a later time, you lose ground in your comprehension and planning abilities and it takes you a significant amount of time to get back to where you were before you left the task.

For example, have you ever been engrossed in a really good book, only to be interrupted and have to put it down suddenly. You're like that dog in the movie "Up" who is present to the person speaking to him one minute and then he sees a "SQUIRREL!" (What is it about squirrels, anyway?) And all of his focus was lost. It works the same for you. When you pick up the book again a day or two later you find yourself reading several pages before the page you stopped on because you need to locate your place in the story again.

It works the same way with a project you're working on, only you're the one who is responsible for writing the pages (delivering the work product). No one has done the heavy lifting for you. It's up to you to bring the brain power, inspiration, and focus to the project or task. If you don't know what you were thinking when you stopped mid-stream, you'll be forced to review what you've done and hope that you can figure out where you left off and where to go from there.

Instead, hit a virtual "pause button." Leave yourself a "pass down" reminder so that you can skip that frustrating, time-consuming, and useless step and instead get right back to business. A "pass down" reminder should be brief, easy to comprehend, and directed at positioning your mind to be exactly where it was when you walked away. A good way to write a good "pass down" is to imagine that you ran off to that Caribbean getaway you keep dreaming of hiding out at and your replacement needs to jump right in and make it happen. What would you tell him to do next? Just a couple of quick guiding statements are necessary. Since I'm all about the implementation, I'm going to offer testimony to it along with giving you the nuts and bolts.

When I was writing my dissertation in pursuit of my doctorate, I needed all the help I could get. For those of you who are unfamiliar with a dissertation, it's basically a book. More specifically, it is a research proposal followed by a description of the research project and research results. It has to be reviewed painstakingly by your academic advisor and a committee of professors and professionals. It puts your academic muscles to the stretch test, even under the best of circumstances.

Well, being six months post-partum with a toddler in tow was clearly not the best of circumstances. My youngest was still nursing and, in total support of my dissertation (not!), she started nursing almost round the clock just as the heavy lifting of writing was setting in.

I believe that she was regressing because I was being pulled in other directions and she was having none of it. She hasn't changed much since, her hair just got longer and her vocabulary more extensive. And my three-year-old was full of her own challenges. She needed Mommy, too, so I was scatterbrained to say the very least. I had one pulling on my pant leg and the other on my, well, shirt.

Oh, and did I mention that I was running my own business out of my house and writing a dissertation while taking care of my daughters? Insanity. If there was any span of my life that I could have used drugs, it was this six-month stretch. I say all of this not to tug on your compassionate heartstrings but to say that if this focus approach worked for me, it sure as heck will work for you.

Every time I had to put my dissertation down to attend to something else, I left myself a note ("pass down") right there in the document stating what I was about to start working on, what I was thinking, and the next couple of things I wanted to look at. It took all of about 60 seconds, which was tolerable to my little ones (well, some moments more than others). When I returned to the computer, I was able to pick up where I left off and move forward.

The interruptions didn't cost me much time. And that was critical given how often I got interrupted and taken off my task. And I was a more relaxed Mommy because I knew that focusing on my children wasn't going to make things go badly for me and cause me additional work. Well, at least that was true when I remembered to hit "save changes," but that's another story altogether.

In addition to the "pass down" approach, the other saving grace in tackling that mountain of a project was breaking things down into manageable chunks. When I contemplated writing 300-400 pages on a topic, I wanted to hide under a rock. It was more than daunting. It was downright terrifying. I had to find a way: First, to motivate myself to first come out from hiding, and second, to actually write it. So I analyzed the project and divided it into chapters (each had an electronic folder) and chapter sections (each had a separate document). Then, every time I got time to write, I'd open up a folder then a document. In order to finish that document I might only have 3-8 pages to write. That wasn't so terrible. After I completed each document in a chapter, I folded the documents into one.

After not too long, I had hundreds of pages written and my project was nearing completion! If I had created a document called "dissertation" knowing it needed to be hundreds of pages long once I'd finished, seeing a blank "page 1 of 1" staring back at me would have driven me to quit before I started. Equipped with this solid approach, I kept going. I finished. In record time, too.

Convinced yet? Try it out. Give it a chance and you won't be disappointed. Promise.

~The Power of Now~

I am going to wrap up this chapter and stand on my soapbox for a minute to make a point that deserves your full attention, and it has something to do with my license plate. Yes, my license plate. I decided to get one of those specialty plates and here's what it says: JUST BE. I cannot begin to tell you how many smiles and positive comments I get from people when they read it. And from these impromptu interactions and conversations I get one clear message: We lose sight of being in the here and now. So what's my soapbox message?

Be present. Be IN the present moment. Too many of us are in another moment than the moment we are in....wishing it away and distracted by a moment not yet arrived, just to do the same to that moment once we get *there*. Live in the moment you're in. Focus on it deeply. Focus brings passion, effectiveness, and accuracy to each project. It brings an intensity that drives us to accomplish things we never thought possible. When we are in the right now, only wanting now, we appreciate it with all of our senses. We embrace its power. We notice things we would otherwise ignore. We are completely present. We don't long for the past or wish for the future. All we want is now. That kind of focus is powerful.

Researchers say that we only use a small portion of our brain, and they revel in the opportunities that lay before us if we tapped into more of its potential. Look at what you accomplish on a daily or weekly basis. View it not only in terms of breadth (variety of activities) but depth (how deeply and expertly you tackle a task). Imagine if you could tap into your full potential of focus and connection in each moment. If you could bring the totality of YOU to each encounter. Give an experience the fullness of your mind, body, and spirit. It's awe inspiring, really. And intense. And completely possible.

Now multiply that. Imagine if more people joined you in bringing their full selves and all of their senses to every interaction. What would that produce? I'd be lying if I said I didn't spend time imagining our world with more connection, more presence, and more intensity. When I was a kid, I contemplated a nirvana-like world and honestly believed that I was going to have a hand in creating it. I was young, naïve, and full of odd notions, for sure. Yet, 30 years later, I still have whispers of those images in my head.

I believe, now more than ever, that we create our own world. We make our experiences. We decide what we want, what we will tolerate, and how we will seek to meet our needs. We are in charge of how we plug into this world and how much we invest in each moment. If we simply make more thoughtful choices over and over again, we can create the world (or at least our corner of it) in our image. It's what we've done to this point: created a world in our image. Maybe it's high time we shift our self-image. Make it a little more positive (not delusional), powerful (not power-mongering), and compassionate (not gullible). Wishful thinking? Perhaps. Change starts with you.

"Be the change you want to see in the world."
~ Mahatma Gandhi

Connection & Presence

~End of Chapter Inventory~

"Not all of us can do great things. But we can do
small things with great love." ~ Mother Teresa

Summary: To address how the need for connection drives us and is at the core of most emotional and relational upsets and discord.

Key Concepts:

- Of all of the needs, the need for connection is the most central, but the levels of need differ and cause unrest and dissatisfaction
- Building intimacy takes work and being present, which requires focus, as well as facing fear head-on.
- Some of the strategies for being focused include: Act Now; End Multitasking; Stop, Center, & Move; and Take 15.
- There is tremendous power in the NOW.

What are three takeaways you have from this chapter? What did you learn about yourself and/or others? What shifts in thinking did you experience as a result of reading this chapter?

Takeaway 1:

Takeaway 2:

Takeaway 3:

Rate yourself on your confidence and competence practicing the key concepts in this chapter:

1: I'm so lousy I don't want to respond

2

3

4

5: I'm okay, but I have a lot to learn

6

7

8

9

10: I'm going to write my own book on this competency

What are three things you commit to do (differently) as a result of reading this chapter? Think of things that will improve your life professionally, personally, spiritually, emotionally, physically, etc.

Commitment 1:

Commitment 2:

Commitment 3:

What are three roadblocks and challenges to being where you need to be? In other words, what are three things (relationships, habits, assumptions, situations) that you need to adjust and/or remove in order to reach the existence you envision?

Roadblock 1:

Roadblock 2:

Roadblock 3:

What are three strategies for addressing those roadblocks and challenges? What are three changes you could make that would reduce or remove the obstacles you have?

Strategy 1:

Strategy 2:

Strategy 3:

"I've learned that people will forget what you said, people will
forget what you did, but people will never forget
how you made them feel." ~ Maya Angelou

5

PASSION & PURPOSE

"Twenty years from now you will be more disappointed by the things
that you didn't do than by the ones you did do.
So throw off the bowlines. Sail away from the safe harbor.
Catch the trade winds in your sails.
Explore. Dream. Discover." ~ H. Jackson Brown, Jr.

People, in general, have a deficit of passion in their lives, both
personally and professionally. Those who have their fair share of
passion are likely on the cover of a magazine or on television or
blazing trails in some other venue. That just leaves the other 99.4% of
us to stumble through each day, longing for something that we can't
even put a label on most of the time. The object of that longing is
passion and purpose: To feel an energy for something. A reason for
existing and plowing through the ups and downs of daily life. To want
something with vigor and the knowledge that you were put on this
earth to drive toward it. Knowing that you have a reason for living and
wanting to live that purpose out with enthusiasm.

But too many of us are floundering, simply existing. With no true
north to guide us toward anything. It's just day-to-day drudgery that
holds our attention. What we'll have for dinner tonight, whether or not
the lawn needs to be mowed, which bill has to be paid, where the kids

need to be driven, what customer is demanding a response, what project is over budget, which employee is under performing. The devil really is in the details, and we are breathing, eating, and sleeping with the devil.

Where did our enthusiasm go? Where is the fire in our bellies? Do you remember when you were a kid and people asked you what you wanted to be when you grew up? Do you remember what you told them? Was it an exciting, high-profile, maybe even heroic career? Maybe you wanted to be a firefighter? Teacher? Doctor? Lawyer? Ballerina? I've met my share of kids who said, "Superman!" or "Wonder Woman!" I haven't met a person who remembers saying anything about a life spent "getting through each day."

No, that wasn't for you! You wanted fun, intrigue, excitement, reward, happiness, and two more elements that you probably couldn't name way back then: purpose and passion. You wanted to exist for a reason. You wanted to bring value to the world. You wanted to entertain or help others through doing what you do best, by sharing your passion for something. To you, the possibilities were endless and happiness was not something that you strived for, it's something you got if you wanted it and put your heart into it. The world was your oyster.

Were you so naïve or have we lost something along the way? My money is on option number two. We forgot how to hold onto our passion. We lost our belief that we are all equipped for joy and celebration. We ignored our vision for a life of freedom and opportunity and replaced it with commitments and obligations that tethered us to an existence, not a life.

~What Do You Want?~

An existence. Is that all that you want? Is that truly what you want to have for as long as you're still here on this planet? Tomorrow is promised to no one. When I went through my own near-death experience, I assessed my life. Being forced to acknowledge my own mortality up-close and personal was jarring, but it gave me a sense of how far off the mark my life was. I was compromising my own essence for the <u>appearance</u> of happiness and fulfillment. I was neither happy nor fulfilled. I'd sold out.

Once I realized that my time on Earth was truly limited (and maybe even severely limited), I woke up and I took inventory. I made changes and shifted my thinking. I began a better relationship with myself and the ones I loved. I figured out what I could do for a living that was a life and not a chore. I set my sights on doing more things that would put more of me and my essence into the world, for its benefit. And you can do these things, too.

What's that saying? "Today is the first day of the rest of your life." It surely is. So what are you going to do with today? How are you going to light that fire in your belly to move you forward? How are you going to motivate yourself to find your purpose and your passion? Will you take on that challenge? Or are you going to continue to sell out and be checked out in your own life? No one can live it for you except you.

~Passion and Purpose~

Passion requires having a purpose; loving something and wanting to see it succeed, expand, and take up more space in the world. Your purpose could be highly interpersonal and focused on relationships, (like teaching or being a parent) or more focused on results (like inventing things or writing). When you have a purpose, you plug into the energy that is available in the Universe, just like an electrical current. You are literally conducting energy. People who hear you share your purpose say things like, "you just lit up" or "you're on fire."

Some of us are actually attentive enough to literally feel your energy and we are energized. We want to carry that energy into the world and do something with it. Imagine a world with more passionate people and the multiplier effect produced, sending currents of inspiration, initiative, and connection everywhere. What the world truly needs is more passionate people. So how do you grab ahold of your passion? It's easy: Start with your purpose.

~Figuring Out Your Purpose~

"Your purpose in life is to find your purpose
and give your whole heart and soul to it."
~ Gautama Buddha

Before you can get passionate about much of anything you need to get clarity on your purpose. You need to know why you were put here and what you can to do put more of "you" into the world. As I was writing this book, a client passed along a quote that he heard that went something like this, "Hell is getting to Heaven and being shown who you could have been if only you'd better used the gifts you were given." This was a "WOW" moment for me.

Pause on this message for a minute because it's a critical message. I mean it, a whole minute. Go back and read the quote again then close your eyes, take some deep breaths, and don't start reading again until you've let that one sink in. Need another minute? Take it. Using the gifts you were given is the cornerstone of our lives here. And you won't get much mileage out of this book if you don't internalize this concept. Please know that it'll present some struggles. It'll shake you up a bit, for certain, but once you get it, you will be transformed. Growth involves discomfort, but it is worth it.

Do you know what your gifts are? Do you have any idea what you're supposed to be doing here except breathing in and out air and taking up space on this crowded planet of ours? Maybe you stumbled into a moment when you knew with clarity what you were put here to do and to be? For those of you who have, congratulations! That is rare and special. For those of you who haven't, get ready. You're about to discover it. If you already know, well, please bear with me because I might challenge your assumptions…so follow me.

In the space below, write down some things about you that you are good at, enjoy doing, are sought out for by friends and colleagues as skills and talents, etc. These can be tangible things (e.g., "fixing things" and "organizing projects") or intangible things (e.g., "understanding people" and "inspiring others"). Don't judge them. Just let the thoughts flow.

My Gifts Are:

1.

2.

3.

4.

5.

"Pleasure in the job puts perfection in the work."
~ Aristotle

I was sitting in the local coffee and lunch hot spot in my town, waiting on professional contact I'd made so we could "talk shop" and see if our businesses could work well together. An older gentleman was walking past me and as he saw me sitting alone and fiercely taking notes, he stopped and said, "Work, work, work." And his tone wasn't like the seven dwarfs with a spring in his step and a whistle on his lips. No, this was the mantra of a man who saw work as burden and distraction from "real" life. I looked at him, and in my incurably optimistic tone, said, "YES! I'm so blessed to be able to work, and to love what I do!"

He stopped short, intrigued, I'm sure, since most people would have nodded at him and grumbled, "Yeah" and gone right back to the pain of their project. My response surprised him. To satisfy his curiosity, he asked me what I did for a living. I said, "I help people find their passion and purpose so that they can live more authentically, communicate more openly, and resolve their conflict more healthfully."

It seems this sounded pretty cool to him because his face lit up like the Fourth of July and he immediately shared a story about his wife and how miserable she was in her job and how she could really use some help. We spoke for another minute or two and I shared some advice and tidbits (and my business card) for his wife's benefit until the person I was scheduled to meet with arrived.

Do you have a job that you could speak about like that? Have you ever had a job like that? What made it different from the others? What was the mission of your job? Was it consistent with what you wanted to put into the world? Did you understand your mission and like it? Was it easy to get up in the morning to go to work? Did you sometimes feel guilty calling it "work?"

The reason I was able to knock this guy's mental socks off with my enthusiasm was because I am thoroughly committed to the mission of my work and I am sincerely passionate about what I do. In order to have passion flowing through you and energizing your spirit, you need to live and work with a purpose. I can't tell you how many people I run into that do not have a firm grasp of the mission for which they are investing 40, 50, 60, 70 or more hours a week of their lives. Do you?

And this isn't just the underlings in a company. I'm even talking about people at the executive level. How can you get to where you're going if you don't know WHY you'd even want to get there? You have to know why you're there. You need to know why you're in business and what makes your job an integral part of the success of the company to be passionate about it, unless you're able to be passionate about your job regardless of what the organization is all about. If that's you, that's wonderful. It's a beautiful thing, but it's not the reality for most people.

~*My Story*~

For me, I figured out why I exist when I faced not existing at all. I had held some jobs to that point that did invigorate me, but my life overall was just holding up the status quo and keeping up appearances. It wasn't really living with joy and from a position of abundance. And then everything changed for me. I was faced head-on with my own mortality and life all of a sudden came into sharp focus. I couldn't ignore my soul's unrest anymore.

Like with most journeys, I believe that I was on the path before I recognized the stones that lay before and behind me. For the past ten years, I have made my living as a life and executive coach and leadership trainer so I have recounted the story of the discovery and pursuit of my life purpose countless times. And all of those times have been with pleasure and peace, knowing that in sharing my story, I am helping my clients to find their own place in this world.

In 2003, I found myself unexpectedly but excitedly pregnant with my second child. I was working from home raising my first born, a little girl, and finding it challenging to balance earning an income and making a life as a wife and mother. I had a lot of stress in my life, and I was very sick for the first five months of the pregnancy. When I was six and a half months pregnant, four days before the anniversary of my father's death, I had a stroke. The neurologist did not initially conclude that it was a stroke, first investigating if my symptoms were the result of a brain tumor, multiple sclerosis, or lupus. In my precocious and somewhat controlling fashion, I made it clear to the doctors that I was voting for "stroke." When friends called me in the hospital after the medical verdict was in, I happily announced that I had a stroke. Because I knew that it was a medical blessing of sorts. I was unaware that the episode itself would become a transformational blessing of its own.

The doctors watched me, and my unborn child, very closely for the remainder of my pregnancy, knowing that my life or my pregnancy could end at any moment. We made it through the pregnancy, but then the delivery day arrived. It was a fast birth, and my body was not equipped to handle it. I hemorrhaged and was not staying conscious very long, even with medical intervention. Because of the stroke during my pregnancy, the doctors did not want to give me a clotting agent, but they were running out of options.

Luckily, my body and the medicine and treatments worked together and I came out of the woods and was finally able to hold my baby daughter. In that moment, I knew that something in my life was going to change, something profound and long-lasting. It was going to be a fork in the road, full of new beginnings and endings.

Over the next few months, I left myself open to discovering what job could allow me to continue to work from home and have infrequent separations from my children. After watching an organizing show, I was inspired to investigate that career. I spoke with professional organizers in my market and decided that this would be my best option given the demand for the services and my potential income for minimal hours worked.

It became readily apparent that I was doing so much more than organizing in my work with my clients: I was helping people to realign their relationship to "things" so that they could more fully embrace their relationship to themselves and to other people.

I discovered that I was a relationship coach and clients started referring friends and relatives to me to coach them in all aspects of their lives. I found that the common element to my work with each client was bringing them to recognize and attend to their "essence," the characteristics that made them who they were. In that process, they could then discover what activities and experiences made them passionate about life and that translated into their purpose in life. I began teaching "strategic life planning" to audiences big and small, with the intention of getting the message of discovering one's life purpose as an essential element to living any kind of life on this planet.

This was a new beginning for me: A time when I was becoming who I was meant to be and able to offer my true essence to my clients. As with any beginning, it marked the end of something as well. It led to the end of my marriage. My medical scare during my second pregnancy brought me to value my life in a way I never had before.

And my new career was allowing me to appreciate myself in a new way, as well. This combination of "happy" provided a sharp contrast to the suffocating and abusive marriage I had committed my life to, knowingly from the beginning.

But, I had made a decision to live the life I was meant to live and to honor God by loving myself and others as He loved me. This forced a choice: To leave and take all the risks that a divorce presents, or stay and slowly let my spirit continue to die. It took me years to come to terms with this, but I did and I left and I stayed gone. Every time I feared that I had made the wrong decision, I reminded myself that I could not remain in a marriage that would suffocate the life I was meant to live. This gave me peace, as did my clients who wrestled with change decisions of their own and then used our work together to transform their own lives into intentional, passionate, and purposeful ones.

For the past number of years, even amidst a very protracted and conflicted divorce, I am clear every moment of every day that I am doing exactly what I was put on this Earth to do: to guide, to inspire, and to connect. In my former jobs and in my marriage I could not do any of those, or to such a minimal level that they weren't worth doing at all. With this clarity, I can make purposeful decisions and take passionate actions to follow my path wherever it may lead me. All the while, I know that the beauty of this is that the journey *is* the destination.

So what did I learn from all of this? It's simple: I learned the transformational power of passion.

~Whatever You Do, Do It With Passion.~

A client of mine is a runner. You know the type. He gets up at o'dark thirty to run some ridiculous distance in rain, sleet, snow, or wind to stay in tip-top athlete shape. A runner. Not like me who "ran" one summer in order to drop a few pounds. Aside from weight loss, the only reason I could come up with to run was if I was being chased.

And even then I'd just hope fate intervened and I could grab a ride somehow. He's not a "runner" like me. He's a real runner. He actually looked forward to catching a run. I don't know if it was the endorphins or being in good shape or what, but he loved running and didn't see it as torment (that would be me).

Now, back to my running client. On our coaching call one day, we were talking about the last time that he felt an overwhelming sense of happy and oneness with the world. In response, he shared with me some details about his morning run. He was running and he made a conscious effort to smile as he ran. Not a small grin but a big toothy smile.

If you've ever noticed, runners don't tend to smile. They wince. They grit their teeth. They're on a mission: to survive the run. Aside from having painful dental work done, they look like they couldn't be suffering much more. Now, I don't know about you, but this is not a good recruitment tactic to get other people to tie their laces and hit the streets.

My client is of a different breed altogether. He's not a conformist. He's not run of the mill. He's daring, unique, and, *passionate*. He also observed that runners look miserable and decided that he was not going to be *that* kind of runner. He was going to be *his* breed of runner: He was going to enjoy himself and make sure that the world knew it. So he smiled, widely. And this little social experiment of his was met with some strange looks; of bewilderment, of curiosity, and sometimes of amusement. He even got a few return smiles. The first morning of his experiment he ran further and stronger than usual, and he returned invigorated instead of exhausted. So he kept it up. He's still running regularly, and he's still smiling throughout.

Is that how you run? Is that how you do anything? Have you ever tried dancing and singing your way through your daily chores? No, I'm not kidding. Imagine waking up on a Saturday morning with a long series of things on your "to do" list, and instead of groaning and wanting to crawl under a rock rather than face the list, you jump out of bed with a smile on your face. You turn on your favorite music playlist, crank up the volume, and start at it. You see if you can get a chore done before the end of a song. You be-bop around the house, vacuuming to the beat of the music. You dance while you scrub. Mopping to music is an experience, trust me.

If you have a family or roommates, you'll most likely get some willing help. You've turned obligations into an opportunity for fun. You've become a poster child for not letting life drag you down, but instead lift you up. Think you'll get everything done quicker? You bet you will. And you'll have energy in reserves to do other things. You'll plow through that list of "must dos" and move right onto the "want tos." And you won't feel stressed and burdened. Is there a downside? Not one that comes even close to the upside. Counting the days until Saturday, aren't you?

If you can do your household chores with passion and enthusiasm, what about the rest of your life? Where else could you stand to infuse some of that energy? In your work? In your relationships? Where should you start? I'm a big proponent of starting small and building things up. If you jump in and try to do everything differently, you might not recognize yourself and that cosmic shift might be enough to throw you back to the starting line. Everything all at once can be shocking to you and to everyone around you.

And other people's responses will surely affect you. You might surprise people and they may have been comfortable with you just the way you were. So they might work against you, in subtle ways or in overt ones. Maybe they'll tease you, telling you to "tone it down." Or maybe they'll add more to your plate so it'll be harder for you to be light and cheerful. If you start small and add in some passion to one activity at a time, you'll find less resistance. We don't tend to notice subtle shifts and are slow to react to them. It's like boiling a frog. Drop him in boiling water and he'll jump. Place him in a pot of cool water and slowly boil it and he'll stay put. We react to sudden change, too. If you want lasting change, introduce it slowly and keep at it. You can do this. So do it.

~Infusing Passion Into Your Personal Relationships~

There are literally thousands of human emotions that we have words for, but of the ones we experience on a routine basis, we can count that number on our fingers. Of those, about half (at best) are negative emotions. What's your North Star? Happy? Angry? Do you know people whose excitement is contagious? When they speak about something that is important to them you want to learn more, experience more? People hear them and stop what they are doing to pay attention because the energy is magnetic. That's passion. It's love, but love with energy and enthusiasm.

We love lots of things and people in our lives if we're lucky. But love can be static. Unfortunately, so many of our "loving" relationships lack the energy behind the feeling of love. We say we "love" them but it doesn't move or change or inspire us to be any certain way. It just exists. It just *is*. It's like a warm blanket: Comforting, but once you're warm, it's just there. Passion can't just exist. Passion moves and changes and transforms the things that it touches. It brings in light and energy and inspiration. It's not a blanket. It's fire. It burns in you, propelling you toward that which you may not even be able to see. It can, and should, be life changing. Why might this sound foreign to you?

Because, sadly, it's not so common in our world. Unless it's about a sports team or political figure, over time we've gotten passion kicked out of us. We've been trained not to get our hopes up. Not to be too intense or we might upset someone. Not to rejoice too much or we might get embarrassed or make someone else feel left out. If we're passionate about something, often it's in the shadows, in the corners of our lives. In our relationships, a lack of passion is destructive. The rate of infidelity is astronomical, and that's just what statistics can report on a most private situation.

Why are people cheating? The list of reasons varies, but from what I've found, and experienced, it comes from a need for passion, a demand for that energy and connection. Passion is life giving. Passion makes you feel as though you've awakened from a deep slumber to a bright and joyful moment in which you're firing on all pistons and are ready to take on the world. For those of you who have cheated, does this sound familiar? Did you stray because you needed to feel more alive? Were you nearly dead and needed life support, or conversely, were you energized and needed an outlet in which to dance in that energy because your marital relationship was "dead?"

Passion marks the beginning of many romantic relationships. It fills us with the sense that we are greater and more powerful than we ever thought we could be. We leave behind our Clark Kent-ness and transform into Superman.

But we never really changed. We just woke up. Superman was always there, cape at the ready. Plugging into the energy and clarity that passion provides, we can finally recognize our own power and potential. The trick for some of us is to find a better way than Clark did, because for more than half of his existence, he couldn't share in the joy of his true love, Lois Lane. Can you imagine if he'd been able to live his true passion and integrate his two beings into one? Imagine the joy and peace he would feel, not having to live behind the Clark Kent mask (the glasses, the bad hair, the reserved and cowardly nerd). If he could be all that he was meant to be every day, all day. And not just in the corners, through his alter ego.

Considering your core relationships, try answering the following questions: Why are you there, in that relationship? What does it bring to you and what do you bring to it? Without purpose there can be no passion. Think of the task of making someone dinner. If you want to simply make your guests full, you might cook a completely different meal (less complex, fewer ingredients, shorter time frame) than if you wanted them to feel wined and dined and pampered.

If you're married or committed in some way to a partner, what is your purpose in being in your relationship? Are you all about the gourmet meal to spoil your partner or are you all about function (making sure starvation doesn't set in)? How do you know if your purpose for the relationship (maybe just to cohabitate and take care of family responsibilities) isn't different than your spouse's (being intimately connected, romantically committed, and creating magic in day-to-day interactions)? That's like the difference between chicken nuggets and potato puffs for dinner instead of filet mignon and fresh scalloped potatoes.

Wouldn't it be good to know how your definition of "happy" fits with your spouse's? That's when the real work can begin, to align those needs. To feed the needs that both of you have respectively for passion and connection. How can you do that? The first step is Discovery, or finding out what makes you and your partner happy and what feeds each of your needs. The second step is Negotiation, or coming to some agreement with your spouse as to what you can each do to feed one another's needs. The third step is Implementation, or feeding those needs with intentional, authentic, and caring action.

The fourth and final step is Evaluation, or coming to terms with what's working and what's not. In this step, as in the preceding ones, both partners must be honest with themselves and one another as to what they need and what they are willing to offer. You can't smile and shine the other person on, pretending it's all better or that you don't mind stretching yourself to feed their needs. That won't last long and resentment is sure to sink into your relationship, destroying it from the inside out. Be courageous and be honest with yourself and your partner or you will spend your time living behind a mask and never really feeling the joy of the connection that you seek.

Which brings me right to the "bad" news. Sometimes in the evaluation step, even if all of the other steps were done with caring and willingness, you may find that there is a lack of fit between what one of you needs and what the other is capable of giving. You want one depth of connection and the other person is satisfied with another depth. And you cannot change the other person. Do I need to repeat myself? You cannot change them. Regardless of how charming, insightful, inspiring, and powerful you may be, you cannot change another person. You can invite them to change, but you cannot do the work for them. That old adage, "you can lead a horse to water but you can't make him drink" holds true for us two-legged creatures, too.

Feel free to show your partner the path to you, to your vision of happiness, but don't think for a second that you can make them submit to your will. Oh, they may stay in that space for some time if you insist on trying to control them. For the good of sameness, security, the kids, and the status quo, you might not lose them on the surface. But sure as the sun will rise in the morning, you will lose them underneath, on the levels that should matter in a relationship. Like a dog tied up outside, he will find a way to chew through his leash and break free. So, focus on you, on what you can change, on what you can give to the relationship.

Communicate with love. Come from love, not judgment and hostility, in all that you say. Model the way. Resist the urge to do the work for him/her. Let go of the fantasy that you can make it different all by yourself. You cannot. There are two people in a relationship, not one. If you're going to try to do the work for you and your partner, you might as well be alone. It's less frustrating that way, trust me. Plus, it means fewer dishes to wash and more room in bed.

Bottom line: If you want passion, be passionate. If you want more love, be more loving. If you want to be more inspired, act more inspiring. If you want to be understood, inquire and listen more. If you want to have your needs fed, feed more needs. Offer what you seek. Give what you most want. You may not always get what you give, but you will get so much more of what you give if you give more. It is that simple and that hard.

~Claiming Your Own Stoke~

"Finding the right work is like discovering your own soul in the world." ~Thomas Moore

So how can you capture passion for yourself? How can you live the life you were meant to live? How can you land or create the job and career that will allow you to express who you are and to give the most of yourself? Try this next exercise and you'll be on your way.

Exercise

Think back to a time you felt truly energetic about something. Maybe it was a special project at work or in school. Perhaps it was a volunteer assignment. Or it might have been a relationship. The hallmark of it is that it filled you with energy, with drive, with enthusiasm. You couldn't wait to get to it, to make progress with it, to bring it to the next level, and to watch it grow.

Now write it down. Describe it and how it made you feel. What were some of its key characteristics? How did it bring out the best in you? Try to limit it to 3-5 words. Say those words over and over again to see how you feel when you hear yourself claim them. Share them with others. See how they fit. This is a big deal so treat it as such. If you want fire in your belly, you need passion in your soul. This is the first big step to find it.

This exercise will lead you to discovering your purpose, your "why." And I can't say enough how critical that is to finding satisfaction and joy in your life. So get to it!

~*Warning!*~

You might be thinking that when you identify your core purpose you're going to have to make over your whole life: Quit your job, sell your house and move, leave your spouse, change your name, and maybe go live in a tree. While you might make one or more of these choices, none of them are necessary. The way you live a life of passion is to have a purpose in what you do. To know, to claim, and to live out your WHY.

You could be a tax accountant or a movie star and have the very same purpose; you'll simply express your "why" differently through your "how." My life's purpose is to guide, to inspire, and to connect. Each and every element of this purpose is easily manifested in my work as a leadership consultant, coach, speaker, trainer, and author. And most of all: a mom.

But, let's say that I spent a huge chunk of my life (and invested a heap of money getting educated) as a rocket scientist at NASA. Now that I've read this passage on purpose I start to panic. What does guiding, inspiring, and connecting have to do with rocket science? Rocket science is the "what" that I do. The "why" I do it needs to be my purpose (guide, inspire, and connect). The "how" requires creativity.

Maybe I expand my job to include training new employees or offering talks to tourists or aspiring engineers? That might take care of all three elements of my purpose. Or maybe I work hard to lead my team and channel my purpose that way. In making changes to live the life you were meant to live, a total overhaul isn't required. It might be, but chances are that you can, at least for the time being, stay right where you are. You're just going to adjust your focus. Modify your perspective on the "why." Adapt your interpretations (thoughts) and approaches (actions).

And, if you're managing a team and you see my book on their desk, fear not. They're reading this, too, and they won't be planning their mass exodus either. If one or two leave it's only because they realize that they must because they are in complete conflict with their purpose since they couldn't find a "how" to express their "why" within their current job. And, that's not a bad thing, because one of two things is true: 1) Their job was too rigid to accommodate any modifications to match their needs, and/or 2) They needed a total makeover in order to get close to being passionate about their existence.

In scenario one, you've learned something valuable and can now see if you can figure out a way to change that so that other employees can have a better experience. In scenario two, they were never going to give you the best results possible because they weren't the right person for the job anyway. They weren't truly invested. Creating a culture of being able to live a life of passion through realizing and expressing your purpose will attract the right people to your team and improve your results exponentially. So let the dead wood go.

~Passion and Mission~

*"Don't you think it's better to be extremely happy for a short while,
even if you lose it, than to be just okay for your whole life?"*
~ Audrey Niffenegger, *The Time Traveler's Wife*

In this chapter, you read about how to find your passion and purpose, and although that has a great deal to do with your work, it had more to do with your overall identity. This next segment will address what you, as an employee and leader, have influence over in terms of harnessing passion for its ultimate benefit to your organization. You can feed the need for passion and mission. Feeding the need for passion in an organization is like holding the Holy Grail in your grasp. It marks the difference between an average company and an epic organization. Which one would you like to be in?

So what can you do, as a leader, to give your employees a jump start to live with passion and purpose and to attract the very best people to your company? First and foremost, you need to make sure that the company has an established mission that is communicated to all levels of the organization. Every employee must be able to tell others why the company exists. And further, they should be able to communicate what their role is in accomplishing that mission. Do they know what that role is? Do they have any clue as to how their work contributes to the mission? Not the goals that are set each year. Not how they are doing against the targeted budget. I'm talking about the mission. The purpose of the company. Why it takes up space on the planet.

Disney might have a goal to bring 2,400,000 people through their parks next year or to create shareholder wealth, but neither of those are their mission. Their core mission is to create happiness. If you ask any of their employees ("cast members") you'll hear that same message over and over again. You might hear them add words like "magical" and "memorable," but they all know what they are there for: to create happiness.

Why does this make a difference? If everyone at Disney knows that their central responsibility is to create happiness, you could infer that they are rewarded for doing so. You could also assume that they are given the tools to accomplish that mission. And, that they feel a passion for succeeding, whether for intrinsic or extrinsic reasons. If a Disney employee had a decision to make on the job, the employee would know right up front that the value on creating happiness was above all others (unless it was safety, since you can't be too happy if you're hospitalized).

Decision making is made abundantly easier. Communication is simpler since everyone is coming from the same organizing principle: To do whatever is necessary and seek out whatever possible resources and experiences to create happiness. There are fewer disagreements and more rallying around their common agenda.

These situations illustrate why so many companies around the world try to emulate Disney. Disney seems to have a secret that no one else has been able to crack the code on. Yet, it seems pretty simple: Have a purpose that your employees can feel good about, speak to, and embody in their daily responsibilities. When employees know their purpose and it's consistent with their core values, it ignites passion. It creates a situation where employees want to invest their time, energy, and resources into helping the organization reach their core purpose: To live their mission through their work.

And this can't only happen in the Board room. This has to happen from the custodial office all the way to the corner suites. If companies started thinking about each of their employees as spokespersons for their organization, some of their practices might shift for the better. Let's suppose you need to recruit more engineers to your company. One way to do that would be to get your headhunter on the phone, pulling in resumes from likely candidates. Another option would be to institute an employee referral program to entice your current staff to talk up the company and its openings to get their friends to apply.

What if your employees aren't jazzed about working for your company? What if they don't have any passion for it and they don't even know what the mission is of the company? How likely are they to promote the openings to their friends? Not likely. Who wants to bring their friends into a lackluster company and then get grief for it?

On the other hand, what if your employees know and love the mission of the company? They articulate, live, and breathe it through their work. In that case, you've got yourself some unpaid spokespeople who are naturally talking up your company because they love being there. When you're passionate about something, you tend to not want to shut up about it. Which, in this particular case, benefits the organization because it attracts people who are excited about becoming a part of it. They are invested in the company before they've even collected their first paycheck because they have witnessed how much their friend has gained from working there: Energy versus exhaustion, excitement versus stress, and passion over boredom.

I was talking with a colleague recently and he suggested to a group of us that the best motivator was to go out and purchase an expensive car. Having to make that payment every month would be enough to get us to make things happen in our business. It's an adventurous and somewhat irresponsible thought at some level, yet what he was trying to communicate that what we needed was to stir up a motivation and a passion for our goals: A "why." If you have a need to make a car payment, this translates into a need to make the money to pay it. It's the need that's the motivator.

So what need can you seek to satisfy that will motivate you to go out and set the world on fire? What will ignite your passion? If it's a car, well, go for it! It's not the "what," it's the "why." Don't get caught in the snare of fearing and expending immeasurable energy on the "how." With a legitimate and inspiring why, you'll figure out the how.

And that's the solid gold nugget that I hope you gathered, if nothing else in this whole chapter: When you have a why, you figure out the how. If your passion for a purpose is strong, you have the ability to move mountains to live that purpose. With passion and purpose you will be a living example of the infamous words of Christopher Robin:

> *"You are braver than you believe,*
> *stronger than you seem, and*
> *smarter than you think."*

Passion

~End of Chapter Inventory~

"He who has a why to live can bear almost any how."
~ Friedrich Nietzsche

Summary: To share how passion affects our relationships and our results and how we can influence its presence in our lives.

Key Concepts:
- Figuring out your core purpose is a simple process.
- When we know what our purpose is, we can build a passionate connection to it.
- When passion is missing from our results, our work suffers and we have more stress, anxiety, and unhappiness.
- Our connections are superficial, unfulfilling, and open to threat if they are missing some level of passion.

What are three takeaways you have from this chapter? What did you learn about yourself and/or others? What shifts in thinking did you experience as a result of reading this chapter?

Takeaway 1:

Takeaway 2:

Takeaway 3:

Rate yourself on your confidence and competence practicing the key concepts in this chapter:

1: I'm so lousy I don't want to respond

2

3

4

5: I'm okay, but I have a lot to learn

6

7

8

9

10: I'm going to write my own book on this competency

What are three things you commit to do (differently) as a result of reading this chapter? Think of things that will improve your life professionally, personally, spiritually, emotionally, physically, etc.

Commitment 1:

Commitment 2:

Commitment 3:

What are three roadblocks/challenges to being where you need to be? What are three things (relationships, habits, assumptions, situations) that you need to adjust and/or remove in order to reach the existence you envision?

Roadblock 1:

Roadblock 2:

Roadblock 3:

What are three strategies for addressing those roadblocks and challenges? What are three changes you could make that would reduce or remove the obstacles you have?

Strategy 1:

Strategy 2:

Strategy 3:

"Give a man a fire and he's warm for a day,
but set fire to him and he's warm
for the rest of his life." ~ Terry Pratchett

6

CONTROL

"All the art of living lies in the fine mingling of
letting go and holding on." ~ Havelock Ellis

Control is on a continuum. Control is one of those words that sometimes is met with displeasure, and sometimes with a high five. When you call someone "controlling," it's usually not a compliment. Yet when you say that someone is "out of control" that's not good either. Either extreme is seen as negative. But simply being "in control" is usually met with respect and admiration.

Setting has a great deal to do with our tolerance for varying levels of control. For instance, a military officer is risking the lives of his troops if he is not in control of every detail. On the other hand, you might tend to relinquish control over the little things when you're relaxing on the beach on vacation. What's the difference between those two scenarios? Aside from drinking from a canteen in one and a margarita glass in the other, the difference is trust and fear. The military officer has lives depending on his command of and control over every element in the operation. People will die if he drops a ball. People are trusting him with their lives. And they cannot be plagued with fear or they cannot focus on their mission. They are in an environment of fear and danger, yet they must trust. So it follows that efforts toward control are high.

When you're on the beach on vacation, aside from wanting to make sure you've got a towel, sunscreen, and a cold spot to store your beverages, you can let go of control. You're there to relax and the threat of death isn't looming anywhere nearby. You don't feel much if any fear, and you trust that things are going to be okay. So, your need to control every little detail is minimal.

Well, unless you're a control freak. If you are, as you were reading that last passage you might have even started to tremble thinking about going to the beach and not having every last element of that venture planned out, monitored, and executed. There's no such thing as "relaxing" for a control freak. If you are one, the only way that you can "relax" is if everything is in perfect order and under your direct influence.

But, be honest: That never happens to a satisfying degree so you never really relax. You're always thinking about some little thing that might have jumped the tracks that you so painstakingly laid out and what NOW? What terrible thing is lurking just around the corner that you haven't compensated for? What will happen if you can't figure it out and be in charge of its process and outcome? On the outside you might appear completely calm, but on the inside you're about to blow a gasket. Your mind is racing and you're getting agitated trying to figure out how to regain total control over the situation.

~Fear and Control~

Where does this all come from? It originates from the link between control, fear, and trust that you read about in the chapter on Connection & Presence. In this dynamic, when there is high fear there is low trust and high control exerted. In other words, if you don't trust others or a situation, you will have a higher fear of possible negative outcomes. In order to deal with that fear, you will try to control anything and everything you can, whether or not those actions are constructive or destructive.

Conversely, if you're afraid of something (an outcome that you don't want to happen), you won't trust the situation and will similarly try to control anything and everything that you can to reduce the fear you feel. Control feels good when you have fear and you don't trust because it shrinks the fear of the unknown and somehow mitigates the lack of trust. You are mastering something, at least, so your mind eases a bit.

If you're a control freak, you might want to sit down and take an antacid because what I'm about to tell you might give you some ojada (for those who don't speak Yiddish, that means mental indigestion).

Your efforts to control anything and everything in your path stems from fear and distrust. You fear that people and situations won't do as you need them to do and that leads to an innate distrust of anything that is outside of your direction and influence. If you're not in charge, bad things will happen.

A couple of women I used to work with and I would comment when something went wrong beyond our office, "if they'd only asked us, this never would have happened." It brought a laugh, but it stemmed from this sense that if only we could influence more things, fewer events would go awry. Like that accident that almost happened on the road because some "crazy" driver just cut you off.

But the fact of the matter is that regardless of how bad and inconsiderate the others drivers on the road are, you can only operate your own car. You can't drive theirs. You can be a defensive, considerate driver and not let the sometimes ridiculous moves they make negatively affect your day or your response. And their actions might put you in danger. They might even kill you or someone you love. But you can't drive for them. I'm sorry to be the one to point that sad fact out to you, but it's a fact of life. Other people will do what they want to do and you aren't in charge, no matter how ridiculous, offensive, or dangerous their actions are. How can you move through the world while embracing that? Start with figuring out how to distinguish what you can control and what you can't and shift your focus accordingly.

~Meeting the Need for Control~

Meeting a need for control is often easy to do. Just identify a bunch of details that you can harp over and focus all of your attention on every little thing that you can be in charge of. Honestly, that only goes so far. And it often results in cardiac disorders, ulcers, and probably some rapid weight gain or loss. There is a better way. It requires that you spend as much energy holding on as letting go. If you've ever gone waterskiing, you'll appreciate this next analogy.

When you're sitting in the water, before the boat has started to move, skis on and tips up, holding onto the rope, you're supposed to be completely relaxed and focused only on having the right posture for when you're pulled forward to stand up. When the boat starts going, you stay just as you are, letting there be a whole bunch of slack in the rope.

Only when the boat's distance from you is sufficient to take up the slack on the rope are you able to be pulled out of the water. If you're skilled enough to stand up and stay up, you are then focused on keeping the tension tight on the rope that connects you to the boat. If you allow be too much slack, you're likely to fall over since there isn't any tension to hold you up. If you hold too rigidly to the rope, any movement of the boat could toss you right off of your feet. There is a delicate balance.

The same goes for figuring out how to meet your need for control and allowing others to do the same for themselves. You have to hold on tightly yet loosen your grip simultaneously. I started learning this lesson many, many years ago. They say that a journey of a thousand miles begins with one step. More times than not, my journeys have begun with tripping and falling flat on my face. When I used to ice skate in elementary school, my trainer taught me to purposely throw myself onto the ice. Honestly, I thought she was nuts. She told me that falling was not how most skaters suffered major injuries. Instead, it was by fighting the fall. Resisting the inevitable. Trying to control the uncontrollable. Getting used to pain was the only way to lessen the natural fear of it.

At age nine I had no idea that she was preparing me for life. But I didn't learn then what she was trying to teach me. Okay, I learned a little of it. I'm a quick study but, like a lot of folks, I seem to seek out similar situations over and over again. I always hope it's to learn the lesson so I can be free of that painful repetition, but I've come to believe it's the comfort of the familiar that draws me in again and again. The devil I know is better than the devil I don't know.

Problem is, either way, it's the devil. But my skating instructor was, in fact, giving me control over myself and my fear. She knew that the less I feared falling the less likely I would be to fight it and injure myself more. The approach I learned: To influence what I can (practice often to minimize my errors) and let the rest go (fall into the fall).

~*What Can You Control?*~

"A pessimist sees the difficulty in every opportunity;
an optimist sees the opportunity in every difficulty."
~ Winston Churchill

So, what can you control? What are you in charge of? The list is long and comprehensive, and might even be daunting. You might be irritated that it's all about you and doesn't say a thing about all those players in your life that you'd like to "get in line." Sorry. No deal there. You cannot control other people. Need me to say that again? You cannot control other people. You are only in charge of you. And that's enough. It's a full-time job. You might even be able to use an assistant. And you know exactly what I mean. You and all of your worries and thoughts and plans and relationships and baggage: It's a lot for one person to handle. You really don't have the time to exert effort trying to control other people.

So the next time you're trying to step into someone else's "stuff" and determine what they should do and how they should do it, take a look in the mirror and check yourself: Is *your* house in order? Where are you letting things slip? It's true what they say about people in glass houses; They shouldn't throw stones. I have a little secret for you: We ALL live in glass houses.

A good starting point for meeting your need for control without driving yourself and others around you to the brink of insanity is to use that brain in your head to determine what you can control. This means doing a thorough inventory of what you have influence over, what you can control, and what is out of your control.

When I counseled addicts and their families years ago, we used a model with our clients to help them to work on overcoming their addiction. This model was based on control, which is interesting since once addicts got to us they were pretty much completely out of control. We would ask them if: 1) They were solely responsible for their thoughts, feelings, and behaviors; or, 2) Others influenced their thoughts, feelings, and behaviors; or, 3) Both the first and the second answer.

Over years of observation and experience, our team concluded that if they picked the first option, they failed to see the influence of others and they would likely be blindsided in their recovery when someone's negative influence was exerted in their life. If they picked the second option, we concluded that they failed to see their own responsibility and would not own their take ownership of recovery and move through and past it. But, if they picked the third option, they appreciated the blend of responsibility and influence and they had a good shot at recovery. They recognized that they could control their own thoughts, feelings, and behaviors but that others influenced those very same things. If they neglected to attend to that influence they would surely relapse. And if they thought that they weren't in control of their own thoughts, feelings, and behaviors, they would never successfully address their own addiction recovery.

There are things that we can control about ourselves and things we can't. Aside from plastic surgery, you can't change your body type, facial features, and height. We can control four main categories of things: Our thoughts and interpretations, attitude, behaviors and actions, and our boundaries.

~*Control Your Thoughts & Interpretations*~

Starting from the inside out, you are able to control your thoughts and interpretations. When you walk into a room, you get to decide if you'll see others as being out to undermine you or as a roomful of potential best friends and business associates. If someone you know walks past you, you get to decide if you'll assume that they hate you or are mad at you or if they just didn't see you. You get to decide if you'll think your boss is demanding or challenging. You own your own filter. You choose the lens through which you see people and their actions. You select your own self-perception. If you don't fit into your jeans, you can see it as testimony that you're a fat slob or that you simply need to drink less and walk more.

We can use our power over our thoughts to overcome our fears and apprehensions: To seek better outcomes because we see things as possibilities and not problems. We can also use our control over our interpretations to feed our self-esteem. If we believe that others have failings but generally mean well, we can use our power over our thoughts to work to compensate for their weaknesses. Instead of seeing their failings as a commentary on who we are or what we have or haven't done, we can choose to see others as being human. And what follows thoughts and interpretations? Behaviors and actions.

~*Control Your Behaviors & Actions*~

You are in charge of how you act. Only you. Other people can and will influence you, but it's your choice how you behave. You get to decide how you will operate in the world. Your history may influence you, and your circle of relationships may contribute by reinforcing certain actions (what is judged acceptable or unacceptable). Decisions are your greatest control mechanism: yes vs. no; keep vs. toss; add vs. subtract; stay vs. leave; move vs. sit. If someone irritates you, you're the only one who decides how you respond. You decide. Only you. Even if there is a gun to your head, you always have a choice. Use it.

You want to feel more in control? Choose to do the opposite of whatever the person setting off your frustration expects or wants you to do. Have you ever looked affectionately at someone while they were yelling at you? If someone wants to pick a fight, you can decide to join in or walk away. Group influences are strong, for sure, but they do not control you anymore than you control other people.

We all have people in our lives who seem hell-bent on starting an argument or getting us to react in a certain way to whatever their latest drama or complaint is. They seem to know just what to say to get a reaction. There is power in that. There is power in knowing that you can puppet master another human being. It's almost like they are saying, "watch THIS." Is that what you want to be? A puppet? Doesn't the vision of them operating your strings make you want to crawl out of your own skin?

So why are you giving them that power? No one can make you do anything. If you react to them, that is you exercising your power. If you let them get to you, that is also you exercising your power. You can choose to react or to respond. When you react, it often seems unintentional. It's in the moment. It's like an impulse, something that doesn't even go through your head to be processed: You just do it. Responding is different. It might also be quick, but it travels through the brain and the spirit first. It is in full consciousness. It is intentional. It is with purpose and desire and thoughtfulness. And it is in control. In control of your behaviors and actions.

Exercise

Consider the most difficult person in your life right now. On the left side of a piece of paper, write down what the most frustrating thing they do that gets under your skin. On the right side of the paper, brainstorm all of the ways that you could respond. First, jot down what you usually do. Then add other things you may have tried. Then write what someone like Mother Teresa would do. Perhaps add how a comedian might treat the situation. Be creative. Come up with at least five approaches, ten if you're ambitious. Step back. Take a look at the list. This is your list of choices. Keep this list handy. You get to choose which one of these responses you want to commit to. When you try a new approach, consider how it worked. Journal about it. Talk with a friend and share your reflections. Ponder what was good and not so good about it. And as you're thinking about it all, keep reminding yourself that you made a choice, and you always make choices. And you can choose differently next time, and maybe you'll witness a different outcome?

The moral of the story is that you are in charge of how you behave. If you're blaming others for what you're doing, stop it. Just stop it. Like your mother would say, "are they holding a gun to your head?" If not, you're in charge of you. Start acting like it.

~*Control Your Attitude* ~

The next thing you are in charge of is your attitude. Depending on what kind of attitude you decide to sport, you can meet your need for control less or more. The attitude you have affects so many things. If you are cheerful you invite others to be the same way, as a mirror for you. When you are grouchy and complaining, others feed into that, as well, and create more of that negative energy.

If you're feeling sad but you want to have a good time, what attitude will put you more in control of that outcome? That's right: an upbeat one. It's like cancer cells: They multiply. Attitude "cells" multiply, too. Which ones do you want multiplying? The good ones or the toxic ones? Did you ever notice that the more sadness you express to others that the sadder you feel?

There was a period of my life a few years back that I was the saddest sack around. One of my very best friends actually heard me on the phone one day and her heart broke a little because I didn't even sound like myself. I was broken and every day felt like a chore. I'm pretty sure I was suffering from a mild depression brought on by a love affair gone terribly and irrevocably wrong.

And my attitude brought everyone down. People looked at me and gave me that sad look, bottom lip puckered and everything. It spread like wildfire. Did it make me feel any better? Of course not. I'd made my inner experience an outward one and shared it like the plague, and it just made me sicker and sadder.

What would have happened if I'd put on a happy face, knowing that I had the sadness on the inside? Would more people have smiled at me? Might I have forgotten even for a passing moment all the reasons I had been holding onto to make me sad? You betcha. My aunt called this approach "fake it till you make it." If you pretend you're happy it won't take long for you to believe it and for the forces in the world to remind you of your blessings. So feed the sadness or feed the happy: It's all up to you.

Think of the effect you can have on not only your own life but the lives of others. It's immense. And it's control in the right way for the right reasons. You get to control what part of yourself that you put out into the world: The image you project. And that image starts on the inside so if you've got some work to do on your self-esteem, what are you waiting for?

There is no fairy godmother of self-worth who is going to show up in your kitchen one day and say "bibbidi bobbidi boo" and fix you. When you're saying all those bad things to yourself, imagine hearing your dearest loved one talking to him or herself that way. What would you say? And no, "but I'm RIGHT about ME" doesn't cut it as an excuse. You deserve love and care as much as anyone.

Your spirit believes the words you tell it. It wants to trust you and make you "happy" so it will do all that it can to prove you right. If you tell yourself that you're junk, believe you me, you will build a mountain of evidence and experiences to prove that voice right. So let's start with a great self-image example regarding attitude so you can get ahold of your thoughts that lead you to your attitude. This attitude control example concerns something that so many of us struggle with: body image.

Example: Fat Ass Syndrome

First, please forgive the profanity. "Bottom" and "tush" are just so much less powerful in making my point. And ladies will get this one quicker than men. Ever get dressed in the morning and feel like you've put on a few unwanted pounds? How is your confidence? It's in the basement. Where is your focus? Directly on your (perceived) fat ass. That's why I call it "Fat Ass Syndrome." And what happens as you proceed through your day and face challenges and random glances from people? You think that everyone is looking at your fat ass. You'd swear it's actually flashing neon and making loud, swishing sounds as you walk. But chances are that no one is judging you as harshly as you're judging yourself.

So get your house in check and work on getting your mental act together. That's a huge piece of what you can control. Focus there. Focus on changing it or focus on letting it go.

~Control Your Boundaries~

I'm the go-to girl with my friends when they have issues, big and small. Whether it's work or personal relationships, I hear all varieties of psychic struggles. The situations differ but often the core struggle is figuring out where they end and the other person begins. What are their boundaries? What is in their control and what is not? How can they influence the situation and what do they need to let go of? How can they get their needs met (in this case, the one that gives them some semblance of control)?

At one tumultuous point in my life, I consulted a coach to get and keep me on a grounded path. After hearing my story, she shared a concept with me that fit me like no glove ever could. When you grow up in a crazy family with caretakers who are mentally ill, you have a tragic choice to make in order to survive. Either you recognize their illness, or you believe that you are crazy to believe that your caretakers are ill. It's a choice that leaves you feeling insane either way.

If you believe the latter, you trust nothing about your own perceptions, instincts, or feelings. You know the truth (they are crazy) but you refuse to attest to it. You subconscious mind knows better so you have now set up a distrustful relationship with your own mind. As a result, you end up being the crazy one, which makes it easier on your caretakers because you become the problem, instead of them. You cooperate in their insanity and become a partner in perpetuating it and leaving it untreated. In that realm, you are abandoned because you are left to be the crazy one and this is isolating and damaging.

The alternate choice is to believe that your caretakers are crazy. If you do, you live in a constant state of guardedness and fear because you recognize that crazy people cannot be trusted to care for themselves, or you, appropriately. If you are courageous enough to confront your caretakers and call them out on their insanity, you ensure that you will be ostracized from the family system and will take on the role of the outcast. Crazy people don't tend to admit that they are crazy.

As a child, neither of these options is safe. It is an impossible choice.

As I reflected on my own upbringing, I saw that initially I had chosen to believe that I was the crazy one. At some level I knew better because I did all sorts of things to help and save my parents from their own self-destruction. A great deal of my harmful focus remained, however, on me. My quest to be perfect was exhausting and painful. I thought that if only I could be better, smarter, prettier, more talented, funnier, and more loving I could change things. I thought that I held the key. I believed that I was the problem, because, again, I saw them as fine and me as damaged.

Over time, and perhaps by bringing myself to the brink of giving up completely on life, I attempted to change my perspective and got angry. I raged at my caretakers (which now included my step-father) and confronted them about their insanity and toxic behavior. My words were minimized and they teamed up, as unhealthy family systems do, and declared a war of sorts on me. They made me the identified patient and spoke of me like I was the damaged and crazy one.

It was so lonely. And so scary. Because, as a child, you feel ultimately powerless to change your situation. I was tempted to regress and go back to feeling like the crazy one because it was easier somehow. But you can't turn back the clock. So I stayed the course and the price I paid was losing my "hero" spot in the family. I was the "problem child" instead. Being the voice of reason did not win me any popularity contests, trust me.

Clearly, I needed a course on boundaries. It took me years, but I made it my personal mission to figure out the difference between helping people and feeling responsible for them. In order to not go certifiably crazy, I had to understand that other people's crises were not mine, unless I let them be. I came to understand the delicate difference between reacting and responding, which became so much easier the more psychological distance I achieved from those toxic people in my life.

When I could look at them like actors on a stage and not an extension of me, life got so much easier. You can deal with difficult people a whole lot easier when you see them as acting out their own life story, their own drama, and not as integral players in yours. You get to decide if you want to allow them to affect your mood: They aren't in charge of that. Do you want a part in their play? Do you want to offer them a starring role in yours? If not, just watch their performance and don't allow their "ick" to become your "ick." Instead, focus on surrounding yourself with positive people, people who make your life better for being in it. You're completely in control of that.

Example: Control What You Can

Just the other day, a dear friend of mine came to me with man troubles. She's a single mom with two kids and she and her boyfriend have been getting pretty serious, spending lots of time together and contemplating taking it to "the next level." After a stressful day with the kids, he talked about jumping ship and how she might be better off with someone else. She was understandably devastated. When we spoke, the truth that revealed itself was that he couldn't be in control of her kids and all of the dramas and challenges that come with being a step-parent. He could, however, control being in or out of the relationship. So, in his fear, he resorted to control.

It was impulsive, yet effective, at helping him feel like he was in charge of something. Luckily for them, he recognized that he couldn't imagine his life without her (and them), so he hung in there. The same thing might happen the next time he gets scared unless he figures out how to direct his efforts at wanting to be in control of actions and behaviors that are a bit less destructive. It's like using a stack of plastic explosives to take down a tree: It'll work, but the fallout will extend far beyond the target.

So what can he control and not take out the entire forest? The very same things that you can control. And the only things that you can control. Nothing more, nothing less. This is it. Your thoughts and interpretations. Your outward attitude. Your behaviors and actions. Your boundaries.

Now before you get frustrated because I only listed four things you can control, see that this list is immense. It's a very long list that requires a great deal of attention and effort. If you're like a lot of people, though, it's missing the things you've been trying to control for as long as you can remember: Other people and events.

When you think about people, you contemplate all the things you'd like to be in charge of. How they feel about you. What they say about and to you. How they treat you. How they perform. How they drive. When it comes to events, it's avoiding tragedies, illnesses and diseases, bad luck, poor weather, stock market dives, wars, and so on. For all of those things, there may be things you can do to influence them. You can take good care of yourself to head off health struggles. You can bring an umbrella or a coat if it's supposed to be rainy or cold. You can vote, write letters, protest, and stay informed if you want a voice in your country's participation in war. But you cannot control these things. You cannot control other people. You are only in charge of you. Only you. But all of you. And, trust me, that's as much as you can or want to handle. It's a full-time job.

So why would you want to take this leap to stop trying to control things that are beyond yourself? To let go of the illusion that you can direct the Universe to fit your agenda? To focus on your own personal power, and nothing else? To take up all of the space in your own spirit and resist the impulse to step in and attempt to puppeteer someone else's life? Can you even imagine your life without that focus? A focus on the outside, on others and not on you. I challenge you to imagine it. It's a life of more peace and calm and less of one very destructive influence: Stress.

~Stress Less~

Somewhere along the way I heard a definition of stress that I've clung to ever since: Stress is caused by the difference between that which we seek to control and that which we actually can control. It's the gap. The events are what the events are; it's how you relate to your perceived control over the situation that makes a difference to your mental and physical health. People are who they are: You can't control them, either.

Do you think you can control a great deal of events and people around you, yet despite your efforts, you can't seem to get a handle on it all and make things move in your targeted direction? Or, do you feel like you can't control anything and you're overwhelmed by the prospect that it's all out of your control?

I was flying recently and I heard a young man headed into what sounded like a full-on panic attack. He was shaking and crying, saying that we were all going to die when the plane crashed. He had all sorts of scenarios that he was playing out about how this was going to happen. I heard his mom ask him if there was anything he could do to change that? He said, "No, that's the problem!" She stayed calm and responded, "No, that's the solution. There is nothing you can do to change it. So, you have three choices: Fight it, trying to figure out a way to control something that you cannot control; accept it and be stressed out for the rest of the flight in fear that the worst is going to happen; accept it and let it go, knowing that whatever happens is out of your control so you may as well enjoy the flight."

I thought that was pretty sage advice, and although the child only calmed a little, the mom laid it out as best as she could. And she couldn't have been more right. Once you figure out that you cannot control something, the best way to reduce your stress is to accept that and focus only on the things that you can control, and let the rest go.

Maybe I need to say that again to you? Let the rest go. Let. It. Go. Holding onto the things you cannot control is like trying to fly a plane by hanging onto the wing. It cannot be done. And trying to will it to be done is going to blow your heart up like the Fourth of July. Literally. Do me a favor: Go watch a video on what happens to a heart under stress, like the stress often brought on by going to back to work on a Monday morning. It's frightening. Stress, in fact, does cause heart attacks. And a host of diseases. Do you want to cut your life short? If you think you'll live a long and healthy life in that state of stress, do you really *want* to?

So what can you do to alleviate the stress in your life, aside from moving to a desert island and living life "off the grid?" Since fighting for control is what creates stress, it's pretty simple. In situations where you're not in control, there is one sure fire way to reduce your stress. Accept the following statement as truth: You're along for the ride and you're not in the pilot's seat so consider getting into the plane, strapping in, following the safety instructions, leaving the flammables at home, and sitting back and enjoying the flight.

~Let It Go~

> "Anyone who has never made a mistake
> has never tried anything new." ~ Albert Einstein

Want less stress in your life? In order to have less stress, you have to reduce the gap between the things you're trying to control and those things you can actually control. And there is an inherent battle in that, and this fighting causes stress. If you want less stress you need to try to control fewer things. To make it easy, there are two types of control that I am encouraging you to let go of, whenever and however you can:

- The control that stops you from asking for help ("Superhero Complex"), and,
- The control that helps others from taking control that you want ("Disposable Control").

~Superhero Complex~

I am stubborn. Okay, maybe that's an understatement, like saying a whale is big. I prefer to say that I'm "determined," but I keep getting corrected by those who know me best who say that I'm in a league of my own in the stubborn category. I like to think I'm getting better. There are certainly worse things I could be and this trait comes in handy. In keeping with my "determined" nature, when I set my mind to something, it's tough to remove me from that path. My former husband used to call me a "pit bull on a pork chop." Gives you quite the visual, doesn't it? I've isolated where my stubbornness rears its ugliest head: Asking for help.

I used to have an anaphylactic reaction to reaching out to anyone for help. It was understandable since I felt that I owed my existence to my ability to "figure it out." The idea of handing over any control of that was frightening, to say the very least. Going through my divorce and all of the accompanying stressors, I realized that I wouldn't survive the process without some assistance and support. My friends have been conditioned over the years to assume that their offers of help will be rejected, so I have been amused at times to witness their reaction when I say "sure!" I have wondered if they may have wanted to retract their offers after the fact, never expecting my acceptance. Unfortunately, they are stuck with the "new and improved" me now!

Why does asking for help feel so uncomfortable? It means that you have a need, or needs, that you want met. If you are asking for help, at some level you are admitting that you might not be able to feed your needs without someone else stepping in. And what if they don't step in? What if they let you down? Not only do you have a need that hasn't been met but you also have disappointment in a relationship, in another person. You feel angry, annoyed, sad, or let down. Or maybe all of the above.

But, in the infamous words of Wayne Gretzky, "You miss 100% of the shots you don't take." Take a chance on the people in your world and see what happens. If they let you down by refusing your requests (yes, you need to give them more than one shot), you just collected some information about your relationship. It's not necessarily damning data, but it tells you something. If you are always offering the help and not asking for it, it might just be that your circle of friends is caught off guard by this shift and they might need some time to adjust to the change.

Or, you may have surrounded yourself with takers and not givers, since you were filling the role of perpetual giver. Stepping out of that role is not easily done, for certain, but it allows for better balance in your relationships. And a lot less stress!

Exercise

Brainstorm your to-do list on the left side of a sheet of paper. On the right side, make a column entitled "resources." Under that heading, think about who might be able to help you complete that task. Maybe a neighbor kid who needs to learn a skill? Maybe a friend who would like to spend some time with you and you could do so while you both pitch in on a project? Is there someone who is lonely who could use some company and might lend you a hand with pleasure? Write down some possibilities. Then tackle that list: Make a phone call, shoot a text, or send an email.

Take off that superhero cape and allow someone to help you. And, in the process, know that you are helping them. You will feed your need for control by better addressing a shorter list of things to do, and you will feed their need for control by giving them something to be in charge of. It's a win-win. So what are you waiting for?

~*Disposable Control*~

You already know (I hope) that you cannot control everything, everywhere, and at every point in time. There are certain things that you want to make sure that you control ("do or die" elements). But are there things that you can give up control over in order to make an experience and/or a relationship better? These things constitute "disposable control." When you have a person in your midst who is trying to vie for control of a situation or things in it, put them in charge of something so that they don't take it from you elsewhere. Give them something to control intentionally: Feed their need for control. If you don't want them poking their nose into project A, assign them project B.

A few years back, I was on a field trip and one of the kids was acting up, wanting to be in charge of where he went and what we were doing at any given moment. The teacher, a seasoned veteran, made the child the "Official Water Bottle Holder" for her. Like a light switch, that boy's attitude went from troublemaker to line leader in a flash. He stood taller, smiled, and walked with purpose. He was large and in charge: Of a water bottle, just a water bottle. But he was "in charge" now and that fed his need for control. The teacher was certainly quite capable of carrying her own water bottle, but she pretended (for the sake of peace and harmony) to need to have her water bottle carried by a capable person. It worked, and everyone on the trip benefitted.

You can do the very same thing in your world by assigning control to someone instead of wrestling with them for it. It's incredibly productive and a whole lot less exhausting than what you're doing now, I assure you. Identify an area of disposable control and toss it to someone or some division and watch what happens when you feed that need. It will be noteworthy.

~Think You Can Control Your Image? ~

The answer is a little bit "yes" and a little bit "no." There is an inherent trap in exerting considerable energy to control your image. Because, by definition, an image is not truth: It's a mirage that leads people to believe things that may or may not be true about you. It's a delicate balancing act between truth and fiction when we attempt to control the image we project to the outside world. Making sure we look good, smile appropriately, dress the part, and so on are good things to do because they help to show on the outside what we feel on the inside and to get for us the things we think that we deserve in life. The danger comes when what we are putting on the outside is not a reflection of what we feel or believe on the inside. When we compromise who we really are for external acceptance, we lose ourselves.

I am a big proponent of authenticity, but sometimes it eludes us. We find ourselves in a situation where we need to put a veil on our true selves. Sometimes it's just for a few minutes or hours, like in the case of a special event. Sometimes it's much longer. Much, much longer. One of the most troubling observations I've made in my work is the sheer number of people who are going through life without letting the world know who they really are. They are trapped behind masks and facades that build walls between them and other people, often unconsciously. As long as the image remains intact, everything is considered to be "fine."

If this is you, I suspect you've signed on to a set of rules and expectations that your family or society or some book you read told you to have. And you've designed your life around those rigid structures, not letting the real "you" out. Keeping yourself cloaked. Billy Joel called it "the stranger." It's the person within the person, the one behind the mask. The "true you" who has been long forgotten about amidst the roles and responsibilities you've taken on. The control valves are in check. It's like when we get our kids all dolled up for the Christmas photo. They don't really look like that, but, boy, are they photogenic?! Are you in your Christmas best around the clock? Do you even remember who you are without the mask?

I have a friend who is the most heartwarming, attentive, want to-give-him-the-biggest-bear-hug-when-you-see-him host, yet he spoke of how when he was in new situations (not in his "host" role) he would shy away and feel out of sorts. In some cases, he felt paralyzed with what he called his "shyness." Now this guy was a master at making other people feel comfortable, welcome, and completely at home, yet when he needed that experience, he didn't receive it. We talked about it before he had a big work function to attend and I asked him a simple question: could he imagine simply bringing his "home base" with him into the new situation? To imagine that he was tending bar and everyone around him was his houseguest. Because that is where he is most himself and where he feels comfortable and *real.* And this visioning exercise helped him, immeasurably.

See, if you think about it, you can never escape yourself. You are the product of your biology *and* your experiences. You are a product of your culture and your relationships. You are also a product of your beliefs, attitudes, and thoughts. Most of all, you are a product of your choices. And you can choose to fill out the space in your own skin, or reduce yourself into a smaller, less-real version of yourself. That's a choice. It's a choice you make every day whether you do it consciously or not. Most of the choices we make are subconscious. Like breathing. We are on auto-pilot with our behavior much of the time and we tend to just float through life without considering the fact that we can chose something else for ourselves. But we can.

~*Then Comes the Awakening*~

Have you ever known someone who's said that one day they "woke up" and realized that they weren't living the life they'd wanted for themselves? It's a frightening, yet liberating, moment because you're forced to recognize that you've been on auto-pilot for a significant portion of your life and now you have to live "awake." You can't go back to being on auto-pilot. You're no longer in a spiritual coma and you can't go back to sleep. You're awake now and you need to start living intentionally and be in charge of your own destiny.

And this can be pretty invigorating. The sun seems to shine brighter. The colors are more defined. Things smell more powerful. Voices are clearer. Your emotions are more intense. Your habit of just going along is now resisting its impulses. You are inclined to stand firm or to challenge and not lurk in the shadows of your own life.

But you haven't done it before so it all feels new and strange. And you may be intimidated. And then the Universe begins to conspire against you. It throws opportunity after opportunity in your path so that you can live differently. And those opportunities may look like challenges or problems, but rest assured that they are there to invite you to break out of your comfort zone. To try on your new identity. Know that if you don't grab those chances when they first appear, bigger and more dramatic options will follow.

And if you ignore later chances, watch yourself, because it may feel like you're hovering over the edge of a cliff, dangling by a thread, hoping to grab ahold of something, anything.

It's like the guy who is in a massive flood. As the water is building up in the streets, someone pulls up in a truck and offers him a ride out to safety. The guy says, "No, thank you. I'm waiting for God to save me." A short time later, the water is now flooding his house. A boat pulls up and asks if he wants a ride. He refuses, citing God's impending arrival again. Not long after, the man is now perched on his roof with water cresting at the roofline. A helicopter throws him a line and the man refuses it, saying, "God will save me." The man eventually drowns sitting there on his rooftop and he proceeds up to Heaven.

The man is crazily mad at God, saying, "Why didn't you save me?" God replies, "I sent you a truck, a boat, and a helicopter. What were you waiting for?"

Don't wait for things to be perfect: You will likely die waiting. And don't kill yourself trying to make everything perfect. Perfection is an illusion. Control what you can, feel that need fed, and move forward.

~Control At The Office~

In this chapter, you read about how to feed your need for control, while acknowledging where your influence begins and ends. Control is a major influence and dynamic in the professional setting, by design in organizational structures as well as by nature in the ways in which people vie for power, influence, and job security. The remainder of this chapter will address how you, as an employee and leader, can navigate feeding the need for control in yourself and others to maximize its positive influences and mitigate its destructive ones.

~Fear-Trust-Control Model~

In all of my work with leadership teams, I review my Fear-Trust-Control Model (presented in the "Connection & Presence" chapter) with team members to illustrate what they instinctively know: That when people are fearful they don't trust others and they take actions to feed their need for control. These control efforts come out in a variety of ways, with two prime targets: information and resources. If you control either of these things, you affect company production and direction. If you control both, you can propel the organization toward success, cripple it and lead it to its destruction, or some outcome in between.

If you have people in your organization who have high fear and low trust, they will, as sure as the sun rises each morning, control information and/or resources if they possibly can. You might see this as something to criticize them for, especially if their control efforts negatively affect you. That's understandable, but there is more to the story. It is human nature to try to control things when you feel threatened because it brings about fear and mistrust. If you didn't try to exert control, you can expect that things would go from bad to worse.

When employees focus their efforts on acquiring and keeping control, things can go downhill fast. A significant amount of time and energy is focused on control versus productivity and innovation and this hurts companies. The majority of people demand to have their needs met, including the one for control. They might not be direct about it. Most people aren't. But they will demand that you feed their needs in roundabout, manipulative, and even passive aggressive ways. And that "they" might be "you." Yes, you.

When you have a need that's not being filled, as we discussed earlier in this book, you WILL find a way to satisfy it, to some degree. Somehow. In a healthy way or an unhealthy way, the effort will be made to feed it. And of all the needs discussed in this book, control is the one that this applies about 100% of the time. People don't like not having some control over things. Some need it over just their own work and productivity. Others "need" to have control over everyone and everything.

Now what about your customers (or membership, if you're an association)? I consult with countless associations and organizations who are proceeding forward on their merry way, doing things that they believe their customers (or membership) want from them. Many of them do surveys and focus groups in an attempt to offer the services and products that they will buy or participate in. The problem is that rarely are organizations pausing on the true, basic, and transformational two-part question: What do customers need from you, as an organization? And, how can you feed their needs?

For associations, if members are pressed for time and want to maintain maximum control over their time and productivity, offering in-person programs during their work day probably isn't feeding their need for control (or connection to others and the organization).

Instead, you could offer tele-programs to satisfy those needs, knowing they don't have to leave their offices to learn, connect, and grow. And they can avoid the awkwardness of those events where they're not sure if: You're going to the right location, at the right time, with the right preparation, with the bandwidth for small talk, and with the time to spare in your hectic calendar. They need control over their time and their energy and they will feed that need by avoiding your programs, whether covertly or overtly.

For companies, you also have to discover what your clients need in order to determine what goods and services will feed those needs. Maybe you sell cars and the number one need they have is to feel safe (in control), you need to answer that concern up front. How sensitive are the airbags? What about the trunk release? Will the drive train leave them stranded on the side of the road when they are with their young kids on a road trip in the middle of the night? If you don't answer those questions with conviction, you might as well just sell them a toaster because they aren't going to drive the car you're selling. They won't feel in control of themselves or their passengers.

Think about it: When it comes to the safety of you and your loved ones, you have fear so you have low trust and you want high levels of control. You have to prove the safety of the car so that they can have higher trust, thereby lowering their fear, and making them feel more in control of possible bad outcomes. Feed their need and reap the rewards.

~Achieve Balance~

"What is life for? It is for you." ~ Abraham Maslow

A common struggle out there in the world is the pursuit of what we call "balance." We discussed this a bit in the chapter on passion. It's relevant here in recognizing that the actions that you are in charge of in your life include taking the steps necessary to achieve balance. It's about the choices you make. If you really want balance, you have to set priorities as to what activity you value over another. And not just say it, but show it through your choices.

And as you read about in Ground Rules, you have to set boundaries and hold to them. And setting boundaries includes saying "no" and "not now" over and over again, if necessary. It follows that if you say "yes" to one request it then follows that you have to say "no" to another. If you want to have more family time, you have to schedule it. You have to turn off your electronic devices and be with your family. If you want to be healthier, you have to make better food choices and be more active. If you want to be more successful in your career, you need to arrive on time and put your full effort into each day. Small choices lead to bigger results. And they are your choices to make. You are in control of your choices. All of them. Want balance? Create it through your choices.

~Influence Others~

If you're honest with yourself, you'll find that the idea of being in control of other people has great appeal. Does that sound offensive to you? It's true for 99.9% of us, more so than we are willing to take ownership of. Think on that for a minute: What if you could get that annoying co-worker to stop creating distraction and drama (or pick annoyance of your choice and insert here)? You'd jump on that like a moth to a flame. We would love to be in control of other people, some more than others and at some times more than others. Yet, saying, "I'm a controlling person" is socially unacceptable so we attempt to hide that trait like covering up a pimple before prom. It's still there; it's just a slightly different hue.

Control, and our efforts to control things and people, is not bad in and of itself. As you read earlier, having or seeking no control is ripe with problems. And the same can be said for having too much. It's a balancing act and the reconciliation between controlling what we can and should and letting go of the rest. And you have to start with you: Focus your efforts inward and being in charge of what you think, feel, believe, and do. And then set that example with those around you. As a result, you won't be "controlling" them, but you will influence them greatly and that is powerful.

So you can't control others. But you can influence them. How? In pretty much the same way that they influence you. Through your attitude, your actions, and your boundaries. As a leader you know this to be true. What you do affects what others do. As a mom, I see it occur, as well. When I'm in a good mood and doing fun things with my kids, they are likely to do the same. When I'm cranky, they get crankier. So how can you influence others in a positive way? The concept of MSR (Model It, Seek It, Reward It) offers a way to help others get their needs met, as well as a way to role model all sorts of other healthy, effective attitudes and behaviors. It's a simple, intuitive three-step process.

Model It. The buck starts and stops with you, so be what you want others to be. And not just when it's easy. You have to be consistent through good times and bad. It's not enough to say that you value certain behaviors; you have to show that you do.

Seek It. Be active in looking for other people doing what you want them to do. Don't just sit back and wait to see some miraculous change: Be on constant watch for it. Ask about it. Be an investigative reporter and follow the evidence trail to see if others are following your lead. Start conversations. Be an active voice in the change process.

Reward It. When you see others demonstrating those positive behaviors, reward them. Pay them a compliment. Give them something that means something to them. Spend some time with them. Financially reward them if that's an option.

The bottom line is you can influence others, but at the end of the day, people will do what they want to do. You can put out an invitation, make the food, set the table, and decorate your house, but you can't make people come to your party and eat your cake.

Seek to demonstrate your power through influence (versus control) and you will make your world better, and that will, by definition, make the world a better place. And if you're still stuck on thinking that in order to have a good life you have to control every last detail, or ELSE, I leave you with this quote:

> *"Don't take life too seriously. No one gets out alive."*
> ~ *Cocktail Napkin*

Control

~End of Chapter Inventory~

"The question isn't who is going to let me;
it's who is going to stop me." ~ Ayn Rand

Summary: Control is a deep-seated human need. Finding a balance between influence and control is necessary to foster positive relationships and support success.

Key Concepts:

- Control pops up highest when fear is high and trust in low in relationships.
- You can control your thoughts, interpretations, behaviors, actions, attitude, and boundaries.
- Boundaries are essential in navigating control.
- You can influence others, but you cannot control them.

What are three takeaways you have from this chapter? What did you learn about yourself and/or others? What shifts in thinking did you experience as a result of reading this chapter?

Takeaway 1:

Takeaway 2:

Takeaway 3:

Rate yourself on your confidence and competence practicing the key concepts in this chapter:

1: I'm so lousy I don't want to respond

2

3

4

5: I'm okay, but I have a lot to learn

6

7

8

9

10: I'm going to write my own book on this competency

What are three things you commit to do (differently) as a result of reading this chapter? Think of things that will improve your life professionally, personally, spiritually, emotionally, physically.

Commitment 1:

Commitment 2:

Commitment 3:

What are three roadblocks/challenges to being where you need to be? What are three things (relationships, habits, assumptions, situations) that you need to adjust and/or remove in order to reach the existence you envision?

Roadblock 1:

Roadblock 2:

Roadblock 3:

What are three strategies for addressing those roadblocks and challenges? What are three changes you could make that would reduce or remove the obstacles you have?

Strategy 1:

Strategy 2:

Strategy 3:

"If you aim at nothing,
you'll hit it every time." ~ B.J. Marshall

VALIDATION

"Put yourself in a state of mind where you say to yourself, 'Here is an opportunity for me to celebrate like never before, my own power, my own ability to get myself to do whatever is necessary.'"
~ Martin Luther King, Jr.

Trees grow toward the sun. Seems simple enough to understand. They seek the light and they find it or they die. And they will grow in unbelievable ways to get to the light. Sideways. L-shaped. Seemingly so tilted that you'd think that they'd fall over. This phenomenon has always fascinated me.

I have a tree in the woods right behind my house that looks like a bendy straw: It shifts from side to side throughout its midsection. The trees are dense back there but they've thinned out over the years, so the trees that were surrounding this tree have mostly disappeared. This crazy tree must have had to grow in and around its neighbors in order to secure sunlight. But it prevailed. Its struggle did not mean its demise. It kept seeking the sun, and kept finding it. And it kept growing.

The tree is just like you and me. We seek the light to nourish us and help us to grow. But our light is not the physical sun: it's another building block. It's having the light shine on us, to illuminate us, to show others who we are. It's validation. Being cared about and valued. Noticed. Acknowledged for what we bring to the table. Understood.

What does it mean to be validated? The dictionary definition is "to recognize, establish, or illustrate the worthiness or legitimacy of" (Merriam-Webster.com). When someone validates your experience they might do it with compassion ("that must feel terribly") or joint anger ("I can't believe they did that to you!"). In some cases, it's in a knowing look, touch, or the comfort that comes from a calm presence in the face of a storm. It's that friend that comes to sit with you and just be with you as you cry on the mat. She's telling you that she "gets" you and that you're not alone or crazy. Well, maybe a little crazy, but the cute kind of crazy. That you're understood and maybe you're in a bad situation but that doesn't make you bad.

You might be one of those people who says that you don't do the things you do for the attention you attract. You don't need validation. Validation is for insecure, needy people. You're no attention whore. You're elevated. Self-actualized. I might buy that if you can admit that doing the things that you do makes you feel intrinsically good, and that's all you seek. Intrinsic reward. You don't seek to have the masses to fall at your feet in appreciation. Instead, you bring an amount of positive reinforcement to yourself privately. Either way, you have an innate need to feel validated.

~Nice Guy/Girl Syndrome~

In order to meet your need for validation, you might do a whole host of things. Usually the things you do to feel that understanding from others are positive (performing kind acts, accomplishing your goals, keeping yourself healthy and attractive). "Positive" can be hijacked, however. It can be morphed into something negative and destructive if taken to the extreme. "How" you ask?

Take "performing kind acts" as an example. Generosity is a wonderful thing and we are called to help one another out, to make the journey a little easier. But what happens when you overextend yourself? Focus on taking care of others, excluding your needs? Not only will you suffer burnout at some point, but resentment will set in. There are an endless supply of people who do things for others with the (hidden) expectation that those people will "owe" them at some point down the line. I know I've found myself in the position of turning myself inside out for a friend only to find that they couldn't be bothered to offer anything that I needed when it was my "turn." There I was, on my proverbial knees, and you could have heard a cricket chirp. Nothing. No offer of help. Nada. Silence. And that hurt. Deeply.

Pain offers to teach us something if we are so inclined, so I took this hurtful moment to ask myself about my "giving" nature. I was uncomfortable when I recognized that giving to others wasn't all altruistic for me. I was getting something out of it more than a warm fuzzy feeling. It was my way of connecting to other people and endearing myself to them. My childhood built a wild fear of abandonment in me, and although I've worked for years to loosen its hold on my psyche, it holds on hard and pops up when I least expect it. Although I can't quote it directly, I'm pretty certain that my subconscious was saying something like, "hey, if I'm nice and giving and help my friends in all these ways, they'll want to keep me around cuz they'll need me and when you need someone you don't leave them." Sigh. It doesn't work that way, fortunately and unfortunately. People will find a way to get their needs met so if they don't want to need you, they won't. They'll leave you, and all your "giving" won't matter worth a scratch. They may be indebted to you, but it may be a debt they'll never repay.

And if they stick around, you may grow to hate the dance you've choreographed. You have needs, too. Needs that ache to be filled no matter how "generous" or "self-sufficient" you are. Having it all together isn't a bad thing, but if you have a hidden agenda (having your actions reciprocated or acknowledged), you may be disappointed. Disappointment, unchecked and unresolved, breeds resentment. It may be subtle at first ("why don't they appreciate all that I do for them?" "why don't they acknowledge my giving ways?"), but it will grow. You can only deny meeting your own needs for so long. Others are not inclined to show us sufficient appreciation that will make up for the deficit that we created by being self-sacrificing. When resentment takes hold it spreads like a cancer and destroys everything in its path. There is another way.

~Feel Validated~

If this sounds familiar, the question is how can you meet your need to be appreciated without going overboard and drowning in obligation in the process? Just like anything, it's about moderation. Have you ever gone to a party and eaten way too much? You're literally about to pop the button on your pants you're so full. Maybe you even unbuttoned your pants and pulled your shirt down lower so you could breathe. The food tasted good going down, for sure, but now you're way beyond capacity. And being that full doesn't feel good. It feels constricting and sickening.

Close your eyes and go to a time when you felt like that. Experience the discomfort. Feel the ick factor of going too far with a good thing. It works the very same way with "nice." There can be too much "nice." Only instead of fullness and bloating, your body feels exhaustion, stress, and resentment. If you ate just enough, you'd feel full. Your hunger would be satisfied. When you're "nice" you can feed your need for validation by giving "just enough" of yourself, and no more. .

When you take it past moderation, especially when you sacrifice yourself in the process, no amount of validation will take care of you. You've martyred yourself for others and your resources are depleted. Plus, people can't possibly thank you enough for what you do for them when you're running on empty. And guess what? You're really not doing them any favors.

Think back: Have you ever been the recipient of a martyr's "gifts?" At first you might be thankful for what they give to you. After a while, though, you just feel guilty. They won't do anything for themselves.

They just give, give, give. If you ask them what you can do for them, the response is always the same, "Oh, nothing. I'm fine."

But they are not fine. They are so focused on the outside and showing their concern for others that they forget to take care of themselves. They forget to nurture and thank themselves for all that they do. What do we often do when we want to thank someone for something they've done for us? We give them a "thank you" gift.

What would the world be like if when we did something nice for someone else in turn we did something nice for ourselves? What if we validating ourselves? Do you think that there would be less dysfunction and conflict in relationships? Imagine if we removed the burden of requiring validation (by our standard and to our expectations, which we often fail to even communicate)? I'll make a friendly wager that we would feel less disappointed, focus more on the giving, and feel more satisfied in our relationships. There would be fewer hidden agendas, less martyrdom, and more celebrating.

They say "charity starts at home." Can we agree to start validation there, too? To not only acknowledge others for what they do for us, but appreciate ourselves when we do a good thing? What would that feel like? Wouldn't you agree that we'd be even more grateful and joyous the more we fed this need in ourselves and others?

Exercise

Draft and send yourself a thank you note. Mail it to yourself. Yes, you're worth a stamp. No, you can't just put it in your own mailbox. Go to the trouble of addressing it and stamping it. The only thing I might not recommend is to put it in your mailbox, stamped. Your postal carrier may not have read this book carefully and might, well, scratch his head trying to figure out what you're up to. My mailman, Cliff (yes, in fact his name is Cliff), wouldn't blink an eye if I did that since he knows me well. But unless you live in my neighborhood, play it safe and actually go to the post office or visit one of those big blue bins and drop it in. Again, you're worth it. And just think of the chuckle you'll have when you receive it in your mailbox. It really is the little things in life that make all the difference.

~Insecurity & The Drama Dance~

Do you have a friend who seems to always have a crisis that needs fixing? If there was a magnet that attracted drama, she would hold it firmly in her grasp, almost hungering for the next "crazy" thing that she needs help to address. Now, I'm not talking about the "bad things that happen to good people" person, who just seems to just attract more than her fair share of mayhem. No, I'm talking about the friend who continually and repeatedly drives to the edge of the cliff and wonders why she's feeling overwhelmed and anxious and why she has more problems than she has resources.

What's at the core of this pattern? Often times, it's mental illness, plain and simple. And I don't mean necessarily something that can be easily diagnosed or medicated. It's illness of the mind, and heart. If it doesn't rise to the level of a DSM diagnosis, it's clearly unhealthy and it roots from a number of sources, most centrally a need for validation of their pain. "Oh, you poor thing!" Whether they will admit it or not, they want validation for being the victim in their own melodrama. Acting upon the world is too scary so they see fit to be acted upon and to create or co-create situations where people can rescue them or at the very least commiserate with them. Bottom line: this is the need for validation gone tragically wrong. Instead of being okay with simply being seen by others, they are addicted to being SEEN by others.

And what's it like being a relationship with a drama whore? Exhausting. At first you might not even notice that you've been sucked into a drama vortex. You might just be so focused on offering empathy and understanding and support (all components of validation) that you don't notice that they are sucking your very life force from you. They are constantly needing you to rescue them from their latest disaster and as frustrating as this may be, you find yourself running to snatch them from the jaws of destruction before you examine your role in their unending drama. Because you do have a role. If you are validating them and rescuing them you are colluding with them in their drama dance. You're giving their drama air time. And just like Pavlov's dogs, they respond to the stimulus of your attention by seeking to garner more of it. And no matter what you give, it's never enough. They need more attention than anyone can provide. They aren't satisfied, ever. They have a tank that can't be filled. They are battling with profound insecurity and are filling it with validation for their drama, not their humanity. It's like being popular because of the clothes you wear and not the person you are. You're getting attention for the wrong reasons which leaves you feeling empty and unfulfilled. Your need for validation isn't being met. Right arrow, wrong target.

So what can you do? Stop. Or at a minimum, slow down. Don't race to their side as soon as the next drama is reported. Breathe. Wait. Hesitate. And when you do respond, be calmer than you've been. Don't "oooh" and "aaah" and match their emotion. Be calm. Ask questions like, "did you see that coming?" Or, "what could you have done to avoid this?" Or just say as close to nothing as you can. It's like oxygen and fire: Being emotional and giving your friend attention for the behavior feeds it and makes it stronger.

That goes for you, too. If you're a drama seeker and you find yourself texting your list of friends to share your latest and greatest "oh, no!" moment, stop. Pause. Ask yourself if you can handle this one on your own, quietly and without fanfare. Take an honest examination of how you got there. Ask yourself some hard-hitting questions. What could you have done to prevent (or lessen) this situation? If you're about to lose your car or your house because you didn't pay your bills, it's not a last minute crisis. You know what your bills are. You spent more than you made. People do it, but it doesn't make it a crisis. It makes it a problem, one that you can plan for better than you did. Learn from it. Don't keep recreating it. And take inventory of the "high" you're getting from getting so close to the cliff's edge and not falling over it.

If you're like me, and grew up in an addicted family system, you may be drawn to be an adrenalin junkie. You may seek situations where you can feel anxiety so you can feel alive. Does danger excite you? I'm not talking about rollercoasters. I'm talking about setting your life on fire and then trying to rescue it out of the flames. It's not healthy. It wreaks havoc on your immune system. It's a form of addiction. It's time for you to visit a 12-Step meeting. I mean it. Go. Before you can't rescue yourself effectively. Life doesn't have to be like that. You can be validated for simply being you, not being the victim in your own story.

~Come From Gratitude~

Want less drama and heartache? Start with being grateful for what you do have and use less energy trying to acquire what you don't have. You attract what you focus on, so if you're looking for drama, you're sure to find it. If you're looking for what's bad in the world, I can offer at least fifteen 24-hour "news" stations devoted to showing you. What if you looked instead for the good stuff? What if you started thinking about what you're grateful for more than what you're mad or sad about? That's a real game changer, provided you've bought into the laws of attraction. So what is it that makes a person innately grateful? I've pondered this question a great deal as the years have passed and I've stumbled down this bumpy road of life. It seems like just yesterday that I was a teenager, twisted in my own grief and anger and fear and disappointment with my family and their splintered lives. I am quite certain that from where they stood, I was an ungrateful and problematic noise that they wished that they could hit the "mute" button for.

As a mother myself now, one of my big triggers is when my children behave in an entitled way. Like no matter what wonderful things they just received, if there was a hair out of place, it made the whole experience an exercise in torture. I joked with one of my daughters recently that I was willing to bet if she won a million dollars she'd focus on how unfair it was that she had to pay taxes with half of it. It wouldn't make her giddy with excitement and unending gratitude that she was a *half* a million dollars richer. Nope. She'd be lamenting about the travesty of high taxes and what she could have done with the other half a million bucks.

Sound familiar? Be honest. When you're asked if you're a glass half empty or half full sort of person, do you automatically say "half full" because it's the popular response? Who wants to be known as the Eeyore among us? Okay, a few. My stepfather was so grumpy when it came to life he insisted on being called "Grumpa." If the shoe fits....

Aside from the health benefits of being an optimist (and therefore the health detriments of being a pessimist), do you think you'd have a life with more fun and joy if you were optimistic? For those of you pessimists out there, I can just hear you now giving me a short list of reasons as to how that rhetorical question wasn't so rhetorical. It might go something like, "pessimists are right more often and therefore disappointed less." Okay. You've got me there. You may be right on that one. But life is a whole lot more enjoyable when you're not focused on the ick and the suck and the messy that life can be.

While I was drafting this book, I bumped into a man while picking up my kids at school. We were both smiling about and celebrating the warm, sunny weather we were having. I could tell quickly that he was a kindred spirit in the pursuit of and indulgence in happy so I brought up what I was writing about and this concept of fighting the masses in being happy with your lot in life. He said, "I know. Why are so many people going through life miserable? I woke up this morning and was happy that I got another day!"

Is that how you feel? Do you get up in the morning and appreciate the gift of another sunrise? What would happen if you said, "THANK YOU!" as you opened your eyes in the morning? I predict very good things. Give it a whirl tomorrow morning, being careful to not to scare your spouse by being TOO loud. Out of love, ease into the out loud happy if your spouse has a nervous disposition. For now, just say it in your head, with a smile on your face.

To do this doesn't mean that you have to be in La La Land and think that unicorns dance in rainbows and poop Skittles. It's just where you place your primary focus. Is it on what there is to be thankful for or what there is to be annoyed by? Where is your sight set? It's like taking a photo of someone's house: you can point the lens toward the house, angling down the side where the colorful flower garden is, or you can shoot the garbage cans on the other side. It's still the same house. Just a different focal point. That's life. There are plenty of garbage cans. And plenty of flower gardens. Which would you rather look at? The choice is yours.

~What's Tough...and Enough?~

I was visiting a friend recently and I made some teriyaki steak and chicken for dinner. Admittedly, I'm not the world's best cook. I'm not the world's worst cook, mostly because I know that there are some cooks out there who could be arrested for abuse for serving their cooking. Anyway, I didn't have the best cut of steak, and while slicing it into strips, I sliced my finger. Have I mentioned that I'm a klutz? And I was cooking on an electric stovetop and outdoor electric grill, two things I never use. Are you sensing the foreboding yet?

I think you may have already sensed that I totally messed up the meal, especially the steak. And with a vengeance. It was the hardest, driest, blandest steak I think I've ever cooked. And that is saying a lot. As I served it to my daughters and my friend I apologized and admitted that it was tough and dry and I wouldn't be offended if no one ate it. Having grown up in dire straits, my friend rarely had steak in his younger years. He shared a story from his childhood when a similar thing happened when his grandmother made a steak dinner. Her husband (his grandfather) remarked when he bit into the steak that it was tough. She replied, "It'd be tougher if you didn't have any steak." Go, Grandma.

Are you grateful for the steak or focused on how it doesn't live up to your expectations? Do you thank your lucky stars for the roof over your head, or complain about how the ceiling needs painting? Do you open your pantry and smile, seeing how much food you have in there, or fret that you don't have your favorite pasta or snack dish?

I remember when I was in kindergarten, my best friend's mom used to tell us that we needed to finish the food on our plates because people in Africa were starving and would be grateful for our scraps. Kerry and I contemplated how we could wrap and ship our leftovers to these poor people in Africa. Her mom chuckled at us when we suggested that, though I think she really thought that we were being fresh. We were only six years old and already we were battling with how to show our gratefulness properly. Wanting to be finished when we were full, yet feeling like we were ungrateful if we stopped.

Which begs the question: Can you be grateful and at the same time still want for more? Does wanting things you don't have make you ungrateful for the things you already possess? The two conditions (gratitude and desire) can, indeed, co-exist. You can be having a delicious seafood dinner and want to have a glass of wine to go with it. Or stuff yourself senseless with filet mignon and still want to tackle the key lime pie. The balancing act is being grateful despite your unsatisfied wants. Can you simply enjoy the seafood dinner without the wine or is the former contingent on the latter?

~*Suffering Mindset*~

Freud contended that people have two drives: the pursuit of pleasure and the avoidance of pain. I've studied people all of my life and along the way I read about this and something about it just didn't jive with my experiences and observations. I know a countless number of people who seem to constantly go after things that cause them pain. Bad relationships, unsatisfying jobs, unhealthly habits, and so on. So what gives? Was Freud wrong? Not necessarily. I think it comes down to one thing: for some, pain is pleasure. And I'm not talking about a "50 Shades of Gray" scenario. There are countless people out there who feel deserving of pain at some level, so pain is desired, and therefore, pleasurable. Or, and related to this, pain makes them feel alive. You could be going through your daily routine in a drone-like state, only to hit up against sharp corner, stubbing your pinkie toe something fierce. You're awake now! Psychologically I've seen the same thing hold true for people: they don't feel sufficiently "awake" without pain. And what is one of the big magnets for creating painful experiences in our lives and manifesting a suffering mindset? Focusing on them by complaining incessantly about them.

I could write an entire book about complaining: The tendency we have to engage in it, its ill effects, and how it bonds us to one another. Try this: The next time you're in a group, share a complaint about something common to everyone. The weather should work if it's rained or been slightly chilly or moderately hot. Then track the responses you get. I guarantee you that nearly everyone will say something to commiserate with you. And we love it. We seek it. We need it.

But, wait! We were talking about validation and gratitude and all that feel good stuff just a second ago. Isn't that the opposite of complaining? It is, yet, complaining is the glue that connects us to one another, the common thread that links us in our human condition. And in our misery, we seek company. Not just for the connection (as you've read about earlier in this book), but also for the validation of our pain. We want our pain to be appreciated. We want recognition for the path we've walked. We want to be seen for our ability to withstand pain and challenge.

You might not do it publicly, but when you've made it to the other side of something challenging you're apt to give yourself a little pat on the back. "Good job, Me. I rock." You don't? Okay, then you really need to work on that. Life shows us so many twists and turns and we have to navigate our way. When we don't run off the road and crash we deserve kudos.

When we don't acknowledge ourselves for overcoming something yucky we miss out. We also show an alliance to the yuck. We are loyal to it. We send a message that we want more of it. "Once wasn't enough, send me more!" When is enough enough? When will you be done holding on to the things that don't serve you and make you feel badly about the world. Can't you celebrate what you have? Would that be so terrible?

Want to feel more satisfied right away? Want to feel your needs getting met in the next five minutes? Stop the suffering mindset. It's ok to love your job. It's wonderful to love your family. Your spouse. Your kids. Your house. Your body. People will be jealous. Instead of apologizing or justifying the happy you have say, "Isn't it AWESOME? My job/spouse/life is the best on earth!!"

I had a client, an independent business owner, who, in order to be successful, had to attract clients with money to invest. His brother-in-law used to give him a hard time because my client would be out playing golf on a Tuesday instead of sitting behind a desk. He'd say, "It must be nice to have *that* job." My client felt embarrassed to be playing golf, and when we met, he called himself "lazy" and thought he was "slacking off" to be out playing golf instead of "working."

After we did some digging around about what practices were necessary for him to attract and retain clients, that nasty "networking" element, he came to see that playing golf *was* working toward that marketing end. And, even more importantly, he realized that to have a job that others thought was "cushy" wasn't a bad thing! Who wouldn't want to golf (or the equivalent) as part of their job?

Work doesn't need to be stressful, unhappy, and unrewarding. Imagine how happy you, your friends, relatives, neighbors, and random strangers would be if they couldn't wait to get to work and were beaming at cocktail parties about their good fortune at being able to have their job?

One of my favorite clients (okay, if you're reading this and know it's you, you ARE my favorite client...feel better?), an entrepreneur of inspirational proportions, used to uplift me with his responses and demeanor about his work. When I would ask him how he was doing or how work was going, he would always respond with "Awesome (or fabulous, or terrific), Doc (his nickname for me)!" And he meant it. With every fiber of his being he meant it. He felt fabulous. He felt motivated. He felt on top of the world. Was his business the best it could be? No. But it was moving forward and he got to do just what he wanted to do and that was bliss. Being himself and being successful at the same time: It just doesn't get much better than that.

A client told me of a story that illustrates this point perfectly. He was sitting in a manager's meeting while they went on and on about all the things that were wrong in the company. They voiced their frustrations, how powerless they all were to change anything and how terrible people and processes were. About twenty minutes into this complaint-fest, the room quieted as they noticed that my client, a normally outspoken guy, had been silent the entire time. They asked, "What do you think?" He replied, "I think if jerks could fly, I'd be in the middle of an airport." Truth be told, "jerks" was not the word he actually used, but you get my drift.

Instead of appreciating the fact that they all had paychecks, positions of influence, a job they were skilled at, and so on, they focused on all the things they could complain about. And their complaints were not directed at solutions: They were just there to fill the air and vent. Did complaining help? Did it uplift any person in that room? Did it translate into helping any of their staffs after they returned to their offices? What if they'd suggested solutions? Commented on what there was that was great about the company and their jobs? What if they had focused on the positive? I'd place good money on record-breaking sales, satisfied customers, and fat bank accounts. And they blew it.

Life is too short to be helpless. You can be a tremendous victim, but why? Where does that get you? As you read about in the chapter on control, claim what's yours and drive it. That's what life is all about. It's not about waiting for the next bad thing to happen so you can add a paragraph to your sob story. It's not a pity fest. For some, but not for you.

You're reading this book for a reason, so be grateful for that. Be grateful that you've found your way to this paragraph and drop the victim stance. If you've been victimized, you have my deep support and compassion. Save feeling like a victim for when you really are one. I can tell you that being a true victim is rare. As you learned in the control chapter, you always have influence. And your influence in the gratitude arena is to focus on what's right and start there.

~The Power of Happy~

Everyone talks about people and their importance to a company, yet a recent study indicates that employees are at their unhappiest in nearly 22 years of tracking job satisfaction rates, with about 84% of Americans unhappy in their current jobs. Is this important? According to "The Happiness Dividend," over ten years of research indicates that employee happiness raises sales by 37%, productivity by 31%, and accuracy on tasks by 19%, in addition to countless health and quality of life improvements.

It seems intuitive that when people are happy at work, sales, productivity, accuracy, and attendance goes up. Yet even those companies that do take leadership training seriously still ignore the role that happiness plays in leadership effectiveness. When people start from a place of "happy" their attitudes do not sway with the wind. They are not seeking external accomplishments to "make" them happy. The core question becomes how does an organization increase employee happiness? Return to the MSR process outlined in the "Control" chapter for some of the easiest answers to that question: Model It, Seek It, Reward It. And, start with embedding gratitude practices into everything that you and your company does.

~*Gratitude Practices*~

If you believe in manifestation, you'll immediately see the connection between being grateful and being abundant: If you are grateful for what you have, you will attract more of it. So create a gratitude journal to record those thoughts. Every single client of mine who has instituted a gratitude journal into their routine has reaped astounding results. Make it a practice to write in your gratitude journal on a daily basis. Here are some suggestions for incorporating gratitude (including, but not limited to, a journal) into your life:

- Write down three things that you're grateful for;

• Journal about one positive experience you had;

• Send an email to someone, thanking or praising them for something they did;

• Meditate for a few minutes on images of all the things you're grateful for;

• Commit a "random act of kindness" and write about it;

• Make a "gratitude collage," with images of the things you're grateful for.

If you don't believe in manifestation, a gratitude journal still works. How? If you focus on good things, you notice more good things. *Whatever you focus on, you have more of it.* My grandfather had the corner on this insight. If I ever complained about a body ache or pain, he'd say, "Why don't I cut off your arm?" The first time I heard this I was horrified: Whose grandfather says THAT? But he added the key statement to that: "Then you'll forget all about your sore ankle." He understood at a core level that whatever you focus your attention on owns you. If you want get your focus onto something else, you can choose a new focal point, or let the world do it for you.

The pivotal point rests on the choice: It's all yours. You get to choose where you focus: What you give your attention and energy to. Why not make it something positive? They say that pessimists are right more often, but they are unhappier, sicker, and die earlier. Grateful people are optimistic. Not self-deluding, but optimistic. After you focus on the things in your life to be grateful for you find more and more things to be grateful for and you start to expect things to happen in your life that are good. Even things that might be viewed as neutral show their sunny side. And you find the silver linings in the bad stuff.

You create in your world what you expect in your world. Read that sentence again. No, one more time. Can you hear that? That what you have today is based on the choices you've made in the past. The choices you've made in the past were based on what you expected to have. And now you have what you've expected. Are you selling yourself short? Suffering to punish yourself (or someone else) for some sin in the past? If you expect good, you'll create opportunities to have good in your life. And it works beautifully. In the opposite direction, too. And don't be mistaken: hope and expectation are very different. You can hope your life away, while still expecting bad fortune. Expecting good things can and will transform your existence.

~*Thanking Your Enemies*~

No, I haven't been smoking from the peace pipe. You might be thinking, "is this woman out of her mind?" If I am, well, it's not for this. As a matter of fact, incorporating this into my daily practice has been a saving grace in my life and helped me to hold onto sanity far longer than some predicted I could. I promise you that this is a vital lesson. It's tough, but core.

And you don't have to be a self-actualized person or pray on a mountain top surrounded by ancient music and religious role models to do this. It just requires an open mind and a willingness to try something new. When you do this (thank your enemies) on a consistent basis, you will reap countless benefits. Your sanity and happiness being the first two benefits. And, the world will move differently and for the better. Ready?

Let's stop for a minute and think about hate. Really think about it. I'm suggesting to downright *dwell* on it. Hate requires an excessive amount of energy. They say it takes many more muscles to frown than to smile; it takes exponentially more energy to hate than to love. You were made to love. To come from love. And, depending on your spiritual leanings, you will return to love. When you love it creates more feelings of love. The same holds true for hate. The more you hate, the more you hate. And, often, the more you are hated. Now, please don't misunderstand me: Love and hate are not opposite emotions. The opposite of <u>both</u> love and hate is indifference. Pure apathy. The lack of caring. Hate requires that we care. We often become preoccupied and downright obsessed with the object of our hatred.

Now, imagine reclaiming that energy and focus for something positive? Can I share a secret? You can. Right now. *Right now*.

Are you questioning how I've become an expert on this topic? That's a fair challenge to pose, especially as you decide whether or not you should jump off this cliff and follow my advice. So, I'll tell you how.

Aside from studying people and relationships almost single-mindedly all of my life, I have been the hater and the hate-ee. I grew up with insecurity and rage (and some paranoia thrown in for extra fun) all around me. And I married into it. There was always someone to hate, a person to blame for some horrid transgression. Intolerance and passing judgment became my hallmarks just to fit in. It was toxic and I literally felt my spirit slowly dying under the weight of it.

Hate is heavy. And it doesn't let you go easily. It wants you to stay and create more of it. Feed it. When I left, it followed me. Only now I was the hate-ee. The hated one. And I still am. I am resigned to the fact that I will always be. Which is painful yet freeing at some level. I know that I cannot change it so I can release the direct pain of being on the receiving end of it. I know that it's not about me, but it is a reflection of the hater's pain and struggle. And I choose not to return it with more of the same.

But its remnants are disturbing. Just as you can feel the warmth of love in a room, you are frozen out by hatred. It touches everyone in its path. And it seeks to envelop it. It is incredibly destructive. Hatred invites anxiety. Fear. Distrust. Sadness. It is exhausting and it slowly destroys the house it lives in: The hater kills him/herself from the inside out.

So what does all of this have to do with validation? More specifically, this section is called, "thanking your enemies." To thank someone, you first must feel gratitude. You appreciate something about them or something they've done. You recognize how they have helped you. You acknowledge that their behavior or mere presence benefits you. That's pretty easy to do when someone bakes you a cake or mows your lawn. It's a smidge harder when they do you harm. When they are literally wishing you dead. Trust me when I tell you that

I know how that feels. And I believe that if I could find my way to appreciation, you can, too.

How do you get started? At the risk of sounding downright silly, come from a place of love when you thank your enemies. Maybe not the love you feel for them, but a loving place. Love, unlike hate, builds strength and energy. It brings peace of mind and happy. One of my favorite songs is "Good Morning" (by Chamillionaire) because one of the lines in the song is "I want to show all of my haters love." Haters, or those who wish you harm and failure, are neutralized by this approach because you remove the fight. There is nothing to argue about because you're taking away their power: You're refusing to engage in the hate war. You're checking out of the fight and deciding to act with compassion and concern.

Did you ever stop to think about the extreme pain that a person is in who is actively hating others all the time? I know I feel the stress of that ire in my chest, my head, and the pit of my stomach. When I feel resentment and a dose of hatred for someone, I feel like I'm being set on fire from the inside out. Can you imagine feeling like that most minutes of most days? That is painful. It's a private hell. And you know people who are living in it.

So when you attempt the mental and emotional gymnastics move of thanking a person like this, first orient yourself to their painful existence. Focus on the compassion for a person who is in that much soul-level pain. Come from that place in your message: Their actions are the result of their pain.

Did you ever try to be your best self when you're experiencing a migraine? People who are consumed with hatred have the equivalent of a body migraine every minute of every day. They are accountable for the choice to hate. But breaking that viscous cycle is daunting and their hatred typically blinds them to the opportunity to be any other way. "Forgive them, Father, for they know not what they do" (Luke 23:34) fits this perfectly. Hate blinds people. Forgive them for their actions that originate in this blindness.

Exercise

Step 1: Figure out your boundaries (see Control Chapter) and be open to compassion. And validation. Be clear and honest about how you may be being hateful to the other person. Vow to release and end that behavior, because you recognize how destructive it is. Let go of thinking that their hate and hateful actions toward you are about who **you** are. Instead, know that their behavior describes who **they** are. And you know this because your actions do not describe another person and who **they** are: They describe who **you** are.

Step 2: Like Batman and the Joker, think of who you would be and what would define you if they weren't in your life? Certainly think of the good stuff that makes you wish they would evaporate, but also think of how your life and self-concept might be challenged if they did. As an example, being a hate-ee has tested my determination, my positivity, and my endurance. Without his presence, I wouldn't be able to define myself and my actions in opposition to his. In other words, he gives me the room to be a better person because I have to be to not collapse under the weight of his hate. And, his tests provide me with a view of how strong and resilient I am.

Step 3: Put your validation into words. Write things like, "Thank you for making me appreciate the loving people in my world. I am grateful for the tests you continue to present because they offer me the chance to prove my strength. Thank you for showing me in living color the kind of person I don't want to be, the opportunity to be resolute in staying positive and happy no matter what you do to hurt me." And keep going. Create your own personalized ones. And leave the sarcasm at the door. There are truly things to be grateful for when someone is a hater toward you. Let yourself feel the thanks. By honoring it, you honor yourself and you diminish their negative influence over your life.

If you want to live longer, healthier, happier, and more abundantly, let go of hate. Replace hate with validation. It may sound impossible, but it's not. It requires persistence and practice, but it comes with time. And every small effort toward that end builds your strength and resolve to keep going. Objects in motion stay in motion, so get moving. There is no time like the present to hate less and be grateful more and that takes action. To hold onto hate is to be in perpetual pain. Pain does have its upside, as long as you don't make it the center of your existence.

~Validating the Blessing of Struggle~

Pain is such a great motivator. And suppressant. Sometimes when I'm in pain, I want to act, to move, to go, and to get as far away from that feeling as I possibly can. I start projects, I volunteer for things, I offer to counsel friends, run errands, and the list keeps growing. I used to paint a room every time one of my lovers hurt me. He may not have loved me, but Benjamin Moore surely did.

And there are other times that I can't seem to move myself out of that pain. I wallow in it like it's bathwater. I almost feel like I'm in a dreamlike state. I know I should be moving but I am at a standstill, blocked from taking any sort of action by a weight on my body and a fog in my mind. For that moment in time, I cannot remember feeling differently. I know that I have, but I just can't access the memory enough to feel comforted. I just sit in it.

And after I've managed to waste countless hours drowning in it and someone or something shakes me free, I then feel even worse because I've now got more and more things piled up on me. Will I ever learn? Oh, yes, maybe someday. What is it about pain that stifles us like that? I've explored this with clients and friends and I've found some answers. The comfort is that we all share some common threads in our journeys.

We all feel pain. We all get sidetracked. We all feel overwhelmed, misguided, frustrated, disillusioned, impatient, and like we just want to hit some magical button that makes all of that clamor in our heads cease. But, I've found through my work and my experience, that you "the only way out is through." You can't skip steps in that process any more than you can leave flour out of a cake. (And a note to all of the gluten-free, organic-only, farm-raised-products-only food experts: Yes, I suppose there's a way to make cake with no flour, but you get my point, right?) .

When you think of a "hero," you most likely think of someone who has been dealt a raw deal yet stayed positive and thankful throughout the trials and tribulations they faced. That's my friend, Christine: A downright inspirational hero. After being diagnosed with stage 4 colon cancer, doctor after doctor concluded that she'd been delivered a death sentence.

As a beloved wife, daughter, and sister, and the mother of two school-aged daughters, she decided from jump that giving up was not an option. So, she searched for a doctor who would tell her something the others didn't: that she had a chance to beat it if she didn't give up. So that's exactly what she did. She never gave up. When her body was throwing in the towel, literally shutting down from organ to organ, she kept pushing forward. She returned for debilitating surgery after debilitating surgery, continuing to believe that her miracle was right around the corner. She spent countless days and nights in the hospital, or barely conscious at home. It was heartbreaking.

The absolutely beautiful thing was that every single time I visited with her, she had a sunny smile on her face and was always at the ready with a question about how I was doing. Like that mattered? Me? She was the one that needed to be given the attention. But she wanted to hear about my life so that she could take her mind off of her own troubles. She was sincerely grateful for the distraction that visitors offered. She refused to wallow in self-pity. And, boy, we would have understood completely if she had. She was overtaken by every possible challenge. All the cards kept getting stacked against her.

There were times that I saw her that the coloring in her face showed a person who was at death's door. I literally cried when I left her, thinking that it might have been the last time I'd see her. But Christine wasn't done with her life. And she was bound and determined to show her daughters that you fight when you face adversity, and that for every breath you are given, that you are deeply thankful for the gift of it. She struggled with anger sometimes. Wouldn't you? Her anger didn't turn into resentment and poison her. Instead it propelled her forward and reminded her *why* she was mad: Because she loved her life and wanted more time and more health. So when she had even a smidge of it, she grabbed it, celebrated it, and envisioned more.

And how has this turned out? At the time the first edition of this book went to print (summer, 2013), she was invited to take part in a study that was all about her recovery. She was seen as a cancer rock star, really. The doctors attributed the "miracle" (and it is that) she has experienced in pushing a stage 4 diagnosis into remission in two years to her inspirational attitude and appreciation for every extra day she was given. She focused on the light that she could bring into the world and the not darkness that enveloped her. She directed all of her attention toward what was right in her world and the precious gifts of her family, friends, and just a simply sunny day.

Tragically, the cancer returned with a vengeance and quickly took her life. Without hesitation, she continued to be positive, loving, giving, and a graceful example of the light we all wish to see in the world. We could learn a lot from her and happily skip the diagnosis. Simply put, a light shone into the darkness is comparatively that much brighter. Even, and especially, in the face of pain and uncertainty, bring hope and a smile and you and the world will be better for it.

~Drop Dysfunction At The Door~

In this chapter, you read about how to feed the need for validation. In business terms, "recognition" is a buzz word that can replace "validation" and "gratitude." It's a two for one, really. This next segment will address how you, as an employee and leader, can receive and share recognition with others to improve productivity, loyalty, and morale. When these factors are high, organizations benefit greatly. Human resources divisions strive to maximize these factors, and spend considerable effort in motivating organizational leaders to do the same. The U.S. Department of Labor found that lack of appreciation is cited as one of the top reasons employees leave their jobs. It's not about the money, it's about the recognition. And, according to Deloitte, 80% of people are dissatisfied at work. Eighty percent! Who are the 20% and how are they surviving working alongside the 80%? That number is frightening to say the very least, yet, being the optimist I think to myself, "boy, that's a lot of opportunity to improve people's job satisfaction and therefore improve productivity, reduce turnover, and increase retention."

In the following pages, you'll discover strategies to positively impact the level of recognition that you and others feel in your organization. And even if you're not the manager, you can create positive change as a co-worker. People who feel good have an innate tendency to make other people feel good. Want to increase customer satisfaction? 40% of companies using peer-to-peer recognition report significant improvement to their customer satisfaction rates (SHRM, 2012). Happy customers equal happy employees and vice versa, so take a moment and see how you can contribute even in an informal way to making things better where you work. Remember: corporations are made up of people and people can make a difference. Just ask Norma Rae. To make it easy, there are three straightforward things that you can do:

- Set the Example
- Deliver Feedback
- Embrace Politics

~Set the Example~

You have a number of roles as a leader, formally or informally. In my experience, the most influential role is that of modeling the attitude and behaviors that you want others to embody. If you do the work that this chapter requires, you will be steps down the path to being a better employee and a more effective leader. When you get your own house in order, you can then set that authentic example for those around you. What kind of example do you want to set at work? Remember back to the *MSR practice*? If you want more of something from the people around you, **Model It, Seek It, and Reward It**. Do the thing that you want others to do, look for it in others with an expectant mindset, and then reward others when they practice it. It's that easy.

As you read in this chapter, giving others permission to recognize others and share gratitude for their lot in life goes a great distance in creating happier, healthier, and more productive people and relationships. Simply put, if you stop complaining about your job, customers, company, etc., you have the ability to influence what is "acceptable" in what others talk about and how they talk about it. In this day and age, it's a blessing to be employed. Validating your colleagues and staff goes a long way in creating a happy, healthy workforce. They will feel more connected to you, more loyal, and more motivated as a result.

Can you share this positive, supportive attitude when you walk through the door? Imagine for a minute the mood shift if you walked through the doors at work every day thinking, "Wow, I'm lucky to have this job today!" Whether you like the fact or not, you are, indeed, lucky to have a job. Now, don't get me started on giving you an *international* perspective on your good fortune. You are blessed. Granted, you may have complaints about things, but you can choose to complain about anything. Or nothing.

If you have complaints put your efforts behind fixing them, but only after you've started from a place of recognizing the mere fact that you get to bring home a paycheck. And go "home" with it.

~Deliver Feedback~

Have you ever had a boss who only came to you when things went wrong? After a short time you started to have a physiological response to an email or phone call from him because you knew something bad happened. You instantly went on the defensive and tried to figure out how to perform damage control. You lined up documentation, created a paper trail to cover your tail, and contemplated how many minutes would pass before you could grab a drink at your favorite watering hole. During that entire process, you weren't focusing on your work or taking beneficial risks in your position. Instead, you were expending all of your energy on protection and not expansion. What a waste.

What if that same boss had come to you on a regular basis and caught you doing things right? Your confidence in your ability to do your job would have been high, and when he did come to you with an issue it wouldn't be as jarring because it would be placed against the backdrop of the positive feedback you'd been receiving all along. Confidence breeds competence. Positive feedback breeds trust. And trust in the workplace is a valuable commodity.

If you're a leader, how would your team describe how you deliver feedback and offer recognition? Think back to the Fear-Trust-Control model discussed in the first chapter: Could you modify your practices to increase trust, decrease fear and controlling behavior? That's a rhetorical question. You can. And should. Organizations with the most developed recognition programs are twelve times more likely to have strong business outcomes (Deloitte, 2012). Twelve TIMES. That is absolutely amazing. So why wouldn't you invest some time doing the dirty work of delivering positive recognition to the people you work with and who work for you? It's low-hanging fruit, my friends: pick it.

~*Embrace Politics*~

What would happen if you shifted your thinking and started being appreciative of your co-workers, including those same individuals who make your life difficult? There is the age-old adage: "Keep your friends close, keep your enemies closer." And the workplace is no exception. Instead of just vilifying your "enemies," take some time to get to know something about them.

I challenge you to look for the good in and for commonalities with those people who challenge you greatly. Adopt an attitude of gratitude for their place in your world, even with the most difficult people. They are there to challenge you and make you grow, so seek that learning opportunity. When you recognize and validate them, even some small morsel of them, you are more open to see their struggle and be able to identify their unmet needs. See if you can figure out what their unmet needs are and do one little thing toward meeting them.

As you learned in this book, if they have unmet needs, they have a source of pain and discomfort and their actions can be traced back to efforts at feeding those needs. If that person was your friend, how would you help him/her? Once you figure out what those unmet needs are, you can use the insights and strategies in this book to guide them toward meeting them. And you can take your own action steps to do the same to help them. And you will help yourself in the process. It just doesn't get much better than that.

> *"Life is to be enjoyed, not endured"*
> *~Gordon B. Hinckley*

Validation

~End of Chapter Inventory~

"When you don't come from struggle,
gaining appreciation is a quality that is hard to come by."
~ Shania Twain

Summary: Feeling validated is central to our emotional and psychological well-being. And experiencing a consistent level of gratitude fosters positive attitudes and relationships.

Key Concepts:

- When you don't feel validated, you often act in destructive and needy ways.
- You can choose to be grateful, even for challenges.
- When you stop feeling guilty for being happy, the world gets better.
- There are three key steps leaders can take to foster a positive attitude in their organizations: set the example, deliver feedback, embrace politics.

What are three takeaways you have from this chapter? What did you learn about yourself and/or others? What shifts in thinking did you experience as a result of reading this chapter?

Takeaway 1:

Takeaway 2:

Takeaway 3:

Rate yourself on your confidence and competence practicing the key concepts in this chapter:

1: I'm so lousy I don't want to respond

2

3

4

5: I'm okay, but I have a lot to learn

6

7

8

9

10: I'm going to write my own book on this competency

What are three things you commit to do (differently) as a result of reading this chapter? Think of things that will improve your life professionally, personally, spiritually, emotionally, physically.

Commitment 1:

Commitment 2:

Commitment 3:

What are three roadblocks/challenges to being where you need to be? What are three things (relationships, habits, assumptions, situations) that you need to adjust and/or remove in order to reach the existence you envision?

Roadblock 1:

Roadblock 2:

Roadblock 3:

What are three strategies for addressing those roadblocks and challenges? What are three changes you could make that would reduce or remove the obstacles you have?

Strategy 1:

Strategy 2:

Strategy 3:

"Think of all the beauty still left around you
and be happy." ~ Anne Frank

CONCLUDING THOUGHTS

"All endings are also beginnings.
We just don't know it at the time." ~ Mitch Albom

Now what? You've spent some time reading this book and thinking about how it applies to you and those in your world. If you're the compliant and/or motivated type you've already completed the activities in and assessments at the end of each chapter. You may have shared some of your reflections, observations, thoughts, and feelings with some of your friends and colleagues. You may have used some of the stories and examples with them to help them along their way.

Did you do the same thing for yourself? Did you try thinking about something differently than you did before you picked up the book? Did you do something in a different way than before? So, what do you do next?

More of the same. Just keep thinking and doing things differently and very soon you will have significantly changed your world. It's the butterfly effect: The flap of a butterfly's wings can create a wind event halfway around the world. Baby steps move you forward. If you're one who leaps, go for it. If not, do a little at a time. Just keep doing it. Don't stop. They say it takes six weeks to develop a new habit. Give the lessons and awakenings in this book six weeks to take hold and you'll find yourself embracing habits that will change your life for the better.

When your life gets better, life gets better for those around you, if they are willing to accept responsibility for their reaction and response to your changes. If they are inclined to blame and control, you may have some unhappy campers around you for some time. Whatever you do, don't let that be the reason you slide back into old, unhealthy habits. It might be hard, but you can hold the change in the face of challenge.

What are you waiting for? Go grab the life you were intended to live. Feed your needs. Nourish others. Reap the bounty that life offers. You know people who never did or could. The sad, the lacking, the downtrodden. The complainers who were stuck so deep in their own pain and sob story that they couldn't see daylight if it was about to blind them. And they're gone now. They are either past the point of no return or they've left this life behind.

But you're still here. You're reading this book so you're swimming in a sea of potential. You can be whatever you want to be. It will take some risks and effort, but this is your canvas. Will the paints you choose be bright or subdued? Will you paint with broad strokes, or refine the smallest details? You get to choose to either stay in the corners or fill your canvas edge to edge. So, what are you going to do with today? Waste it? Throw it away like so many of your yesterdays? Let things bubble under the surface and refuse to address them? Remain in relationships or situations that are draining your very life force and making you feel empty and alone?

Or, will you take responsibility for meeting your needs, adjust your expectations so disappointment isn't your cloak, and put yourself in situations and relationships that allow your needs to be met and allow you to feed the needs of others to your benefit and not your detriment? Will you see that when you and those you care about have their needs fed that the sky is the limit? There is nothing you can conceive of that you can't accomplish when your core needs are met.

You can live intentionally, passionately, and with joy that you've only read about. It's just beyond the doorway you're standing in.

How long are you going to rest there? It's time to claim your stoke, to own your voice, and to be the YOU that you were meant to be. It's time to drop the excuses, put this book down, straighten up, and act on all that you know and feel. In a year's time surrounding the original printing of this book in 2013, both of my parents and a friend of mine died. My parents were both 69 and my friend, Christine, was in her early 40s. I have always appreciated life and its lack of guarantees, but events over the past 18 months have sharpened my resolve to live my life to all its edges and in full color. To not wait for a someday that may never appear. I have today, this moment, so I'm going to take risks, push the envelope, write it down, say it out loud, and make it happen. Are you joining me, or are you going to live on the sidelines of your own life? I didn't think so. You've read this book so I know you've got some moxie in you. Let's make things HAPPEN. I'll expect an invitation to the first of your many celebrations.

ABOUT THE AUTHOR

"It's very weird to succeed at thirty-nine years old and realize that in the midst of your failure, you were slowly building the life that you wanted anyway." ~ Alice Sebold

Dr. Bridget Cooper is an experienced and dynamic educator, facilitator, executive coach, and management and leadership consultant. She was trained in systems theory and uses this orientation to help people in organizations understand and own their role in their relationships. Her core drive (need!) is to help people to be passionate and invigorated about their lives and work so that they will propel their organizations toward success, create healthy work climates, strong and positive working relationships, and happier clients and customers.

Her forte is developing and delivering interactive and motivational training and keynote speeches on finding your passion and purpose, effective communication, conflict resolution, relationship building, productivity, time management, and decision making and problem solving. She has a proven track record of proactively, strategically, and effectively managing high-level organizational change and translating strategy into measurable objectives. She has found that when companies know what their employees and customers need, and seek to feed those needs, companies prosper.

She has conducted seminars, retreats, and keynotes for numerous associations and organizations including: Girl Scouts of Connecticut, Connecticut Society of Association Executives, L-3 Communications, Glastonbury Chamber of Commerce, Connecticut Boards of Education, Vietnam Veterans of America, Gateway Financial Partners,

Junior League of Washington, Department of Defense, Connecticut Associated Builders & Contractors, Hartford Dental Society, Bethany College, Draeger Medical, The George Washington University, USA Weekend, and American Case Management Association.

Dr. Cooper founded "First Wednesdays," a monthly empowerment workshop for women which brings the lessons of this book to life and creates a forum for discussion and growth. For more information, please visit www.piecesinplace.com. She also serves as a volunteer presenter for WIN, a resource workshop for women going through life transitions such as divorce and widowhood. For more information, please visit www.allaboutwin.com.

Raised in New England, she earned her B.S. with a concentration in human resource management from the University of Massachusetts, her M.A. in marriage and family therapy at the University of Connecticut, and her Ed.D. through the educational leadership program at the George Washington University. Her dissertation was on the social network structures of women in academic medicine.

Dr. Cooper been a leader in the Girl Scout organization, President of the Parent-Teacher Organization, soccer coach, religious education instructor, and elementary school room parent and activity chairperson. Prior to her move to Connecticut, she served as an instructor in conflict resolution and anger management for inmates of the Fairfax County Adult Detention Center.

Her hobbies include fumbling around on the guitar, traveling to places far and wide, and seeking out photo opportunities of people, places, and things. She has a never-ending bucket list that she's slowly checking off, and she takes suggestions.

Please contact her with your bucket list ideas and information on how she can feed your (and your company's) needs at bridget@feedtheneednow.com.

DAUGHTERS' PAGE

"A daughter may outgrow your lap but she will never outgrow your heart."~ Author Unknown

~From Jessica~

Hi, I'm Jessi. I'm 12 years old and in 6th grade. My mom worked really hard on this book. Her first goal was to have it published by her birthday in July, but then one of her clients asked for 100 copies of her book by mid-June. My mom agreed, and has basically been on rapid fire typing mode since then. Sometimes she would shut herself in the sunroom for hours at a time, just her, her laptop, and the occasional pet. We'd often come in to see her with her head thrown back, hands covering her face. This is what she called "writing constipation." But somehow she kept going, and by early May she had sent out copies of her rough draft to her friends for suggestions. Once she received the suggestions, she dove in again. Edit, Revise, Eat, Repeat. She took every suggestion into consideration, and valued everyone's opinion. Somehow, in all this mess, she still found time for us. I love my mom very much, and I don't know what I'd do without her, although she can be annoying at times. ☺

~From Elena~

I witnessed my mom writing her book. A lot. It took away from our time together, but without all of her hard work and dedication, her book might have been horrible. My mom is a coach and trainer. She changes people's lives for the better. She changed mine for the better, too. I cherish my mom's relationship with me and I love her. She's amazing. ♡ ☺

* page left unchanged from first edition, 2013